Knowing where we stand

Knowing where we stand

The message of John's epistles

Peter Barnes

 EVANGELICAL PRESS

EVANGELICAL PRESS
Grange Close, Faverdale North Industrial Estate, Darlington,
Co. Durham, DL3 0PH, England

First published 1998

British Library Cataloguing in Publication Data available

ISBN 0 85234 414 7

Printed and bound in Great Britain by Creative Print and Design,
Ebbw Vale

Contents

Page

1 John

1 John: An introduction 7
1. The incarnate Word (1:1-4) 13
2. God is light (1:5-7) 19
3. Dealing with sin (1:8 – 2:2) 24
4. Two tests (2:3-11) 32
5. The Christian and the world (2:12-17) 40
6. Beware of antichrists! (2:18-27) 47
7. Living in God's family (2:28 – 3:3) 55
8. The child of God and sin (3:4-10) 63
9. Love one another (3:11-18) 70
10. Dealing with doubt (3:19-24) 76
11. Testing the spirits (4:1-6) 84
12. Love is of God (4:7-21) 94
13. Summarizing the three tests (5:1-5) 102
14. Belief and unbelief (5:6-12) 109
15. Assurance in the Christian life (5:13-17) 115
16. Knowing where we stand (5:18-21) 122

2 John

2 John: An introduction 129
17. Fellowship in the truth; confronting falsehood
    (1-13) 131

3 John

3 John: An introduction   141

18.   Contrasting testimonies (1-14)   143

Notes   154

1 John:
An introduction

At first sight John's first letter does not seem much like the sort of letter we would write — the apostle John does not mention his own name, and he does not say to whom he is writing. He begins abruptly with statements about the Word of life, and finishes just as abruptly with a warning that his readers should keep themselves from idols. The letter does not develop its argument in the consecutive way that other New Testament epistles do (e.g. Romans or Ephesians). David Jackman is not the only commentator to compare its structure to a spiral staircase.[1] When our family was reading the First Epistle of John at the breakfast table some time back, one of my daughters, Heather (then aged about eight), once tried to call a temporary halt to proceedings by pointing out, 'We have read that before.' We had not, but John does repeat each of his motifs (for example, love, obedience, belief) a number of times. Back in 1912 Canon A. E. Brooke even considered that 'Perhaps the attempt to analyse the Epistle should be abandoned as useless.'[2] Dr Martyn Lloyd-Jones characterized John as more like a poet than a logician, although he believed that the apostle was nevertheless logical.[3]

Perhaps 1 John might be compared to a musical score, in which several motifs recur a number of times. For example,

John raises the issue of a right belief in Christ in 1:1-4, and returns to it in 2:18-27; 4:1-3 and 5:5-12. In 1:5 - 2:2 he deals with sin and obedience, and returns to this motif in 2:28-29; 3:3-10 and 5:16-17. The issue of loving the brethren is raised in 2:7-11 and repeated in 3:11-18 and 4:7 - 5:3. In each case the motif is developed a little more, while in 1 John 3:22-23 the three motifs of belief, obedience and love are joined together in one harmonious whole: 'And whatever we ask we receive from him, because we keep his commandments and do those things that are pleasing in his sight. And this is his commandment: that we should believe on the name of his Son Jesus Christ and love one another, as he gave us commandment.'

When compared to other epistles in the New Testament, 1 John appears to be a circular letter or a treatise — like the book of Hebrews — rather than an apostolic letter to an individual church (such as Paul's letter to the Romans) or to a person (such as his letter to Philemon). Yet it is not just a theological treatise, because John writes very affectionately to his readers as his 'little children' (2:1,12,18,28; 4:4; 5:21). It is a personal letter and his readers are those whom he calls his 'beloved' (2:7 [in the Greek]; 3:2,21; 4:1,7,11). Paradoxically, the letter is so personal that he does not have to mention his own name (in 2 and 3 John he refers to himself simply as 'the elder').

Irenaeus, the Bishop of Lyons in the latter half of the second century, said that the apostle John lived to an advanced age. He was probably the last of the apostles to leave this earthly life. Hence he wrote to counter a situation that had arisen in a church, or perhaps a number of churches, probably in Asia (the western part of what we now call Turkey). We know that there had been a split in the church, and that a number of people had left because they thought their version of Christianity was an improvement on what the apostles had taught (see 1 John 2:19). The people that were left were no doubt feeling a little discouraged and in need of some reassurance. They must have thought to themselves: 'How do we know we are on the right track? Perhaps the ones who left are right after all.'

The problem was that those who left did not walk out because they did not get their way over the colour of the pews, or because the church up the road had a louder band. The people who left were Docetists, or had adopted an early form of Gnosticism. (To maintain a correct historical perspective, we need to remember that full-blown Gnosticism seems to have emerged only in the second century.)

The word 'Docetist' comes from the Greek word *dokeo* which means 'I think', 'I seem' or 'I appear'. In 1 Corinthians 12:22 Paul uses this word when he writes of those members of the body which '*seem* to be weaker' but which 'are necessary'. In the case of the Docetists, they taught that Christ *appeared* to be a man but was not truly human. Early in the second century Ignatius of Antioch wrote vigorously against one (whom he refused to name) who, in Ignatius' view, 'blasphemes my Lord by denying that he ever bore a real human body'. 'In saying that,' declared Ignatius, 'he denies everything about him.'[4]

The 'Gnostic' (from the Greek word *gnosis* which means 'knowledge') had views which had some similarity to those of the Docetist. He was sure that the Christ spirit descended on the man Jesus at his baptism, but then left him before the crucifixion. Hence there was no real incarnation; in the view of the Docetists or Gnostics, the Word did not truly become flesh (John 1:14) nor did the fulness of the Godhead dwell bodily in Jesus Christ (Col. 2:9 — the verb is in the present tense). This would mean that Christ was only acting when he ate, drank, grew weary and slept. It would even mean that he did not suffer on the cross or die as a substitute for sinners.

How could the discouraged remnant know who was right? Their assurance must have been at a low ebb. As Dr Martyn Lloyd-Jones put it, 'Assurance is not essential to salvation, but it is essential to the joy of salvation.'[5] So John wrote to those who *believed* in the name of the Son of God in order that they might *know* that they possessed eternal life (1 John 5:13). In fact, the two Greek words for 'to know' are found about thirty-eight times in John's three epistles. John gave his readers three main tests so that they could tell who was right and who was wrong in spiritual matters.

1. The doctrinal test

'By this you know the Spirit of God: every spirit that confesses that Jesus Christ has come in the flesh is of God' (1 John 4:2). John Newton said the same thing more poetically:

'What think ye of Christ?' is the test
To try both your state and your scheme;
You cannot be right in the rest,
Unless you think rightly of him.

The Docetists did not think rightly of Christ. They spoke of Christ and no doubt sometimes sounded like true Christians, but they believed in a Christ of their own imagination, just as many people do today.

2. The relationships test

'If someone says, "I love God," and hates his brother, he is a liar; for he who does not love his brother whom he has seen, how can he love God whom he has not seen? And this commandment we have from him: that he who loves God must love his brother also' (1 John 4:20-21). If God is love, and I claim to know him, I too must love. I must especially love his blood-bought people, but I must even love my enemies. Without love, any knowledge or faith that I have means nothing (1 Cor. 8:1; 13:1-3).

3. The obedience test

'Now by this we know that we know him, if we keep his commandments. He who says, "I know him," and does not keep his commandments, is a liar, and the truth is not in him' (1 John 2:3-4). John is making no claim that Christians can expect to attain to the level of sinless perfection in this life (see 1:8,10). Nevertheless, a Christian's obedience, while imperfect, is real, habitual and substantial. The Lord Jesus himself said that there will be many preachers who call him 'Lord' and do marvellous things in his name, but whom he never knew. The missing thing in their lives was obedience to God's will (Matt. 7:21-23). In more theological terms, what is being said is this: 'You cannot take Christ for justification unless you take him for sanctification. Think of the sinner coming to Christ and saying, "I do not want to be holy," "I do not want to be saved from sin," "I would like to be saved in my sins," "Do not sanctify me now, but justify me now." What would be the answer? Could he be accepted by God? You can no more separate justification from sanctification than you can separate the circulation of the blood from the inhalation of the air. Breathing and circulation are two different things, but you cannot have one without the other; they go together, and they constitute one life. So you have justification and sanctification; they go together, and they constitute one life. If there was ever one who attempted to receive Christ with justification and not with sanctification, he missed it, thank God! He was no more justified than he was sanctified.'[6] These words come from A. A. Hodge, and they tell us what the apostle John tells us — that if we are truly Christians, God has done something *for* us (in the death of Christ) and is doing something *in* us (making us more like Christ through the work of the Holy Spirit).

Not everybody who claims to be a Christian is actually inside the kingdom of God. In these days of spiritual and moral decline we stand in particular need of the message of 1 John. It is not for nothing that R. Kent Hughes has written a book on the Beatitudes with the provocative title *Are Evangelicals Born Again?*[7] We need to test ourselves first to see where we stand before God and then, with charity of heart and clarity of mind, we need to test the claims of others too. That is why 1 John is such an important book of the Bible. With good reason Martin Luther wrote of 1 John: 'I have never read a book written in simpler words than this one, and yet the words are inexpressible.'[8]

1.
The incarnate Word

Please read 1 John 1:1-4

The historical foundation

John begins with vital words. He tells us that the Son was from the beginning, but that he revealed himself in human history, and that the apostles had heard, seen and touched him. The Christian faith is not just about ideas. It does not matter too much when Confucius or Buddha lived, nor how they died; what matters is their teaching; not so with Christianity. When the apostle Paul reminded the Corinthians of what he had delivered to them first of all, he spoke of Christ who died for our sins according to the Scriptures, of his burial and his rising from the dead on the third day according to the Scriptures (1 Cor. 15:3-4). The Christian faith is not simply a set of ideas about daily living; it is the proclamation of Christ and his coming into the world as a fact of history.

The Son of God existed from the beginning with the Father. He was **'that which was from the beginning'** (1:1)[1] and **'with the Father'** (1:2). Although John does not employ identical phrasing, he is quite deliberately echoing the opening words of his own Gospel: 'In the beginning was the Word, and the Word was with God, and the Word was God' (John 1:1), which in turn was echoing Genesis 1:1: 'In the beginning God created the heavens and the earth.' We live in an age when hardly a day goes past without the deity of Christ being denied by some bishop or academic theologian. Christ is portrayed as only a man — at most as a man who reveals God to us. But Scripture tells us that the Son is one with the Father. He is not a man amongst men; he is the Eternal One who existed from the beginning.

The Eternal One did not remain in heaven but became incarnate. John says that **'The life was manifested'** (1:2). The New International Version says, 'The life appeared,' while the Jerusalem Bible translates it as 'That life was made visible'. The Eternal One from heaven took the physical form of a man. He did not simply dwell in the body of a man, but became a man. As John later warned, 'Every spirit that confesses that Jesus Christ has come in the flesh is of God' (4:2). According to Irenaeus, John once met the Gnostic Cerinthus in the bathhouse at Ephesus and immediately fled because Cerinthus was one who denied Christ's incarnation. Like many in the New Age movement today, Cerinthus thought that the divine Christ descended on the man Jesus at his baptism, and then left him before Jesus suffered on the cross. The Christian faith, however, proclaims the reality of the incarnation. We cannot see God because he is Spirit (John 4:24), but God has become man in Christ Jesus.

This is the central claim of the Christian faith. Take away this truth, and the whole of Christianity falls to pieces — Christ's teachings, his miracles, his death for sinners, his resurrection and his promises to raise the dead, to forgive sinners who have faith in him and to judge the world. Every word he uttered and every deed he undertook rest upon the premise of his being the God-man. If Christ is not the Eternal One made man, he is the most audacious deceiver who ever lived. Confucius and Buddha never claimed to be God in the flesh. Christ did. The foundation of the Christian faith is the God-man Jesus Christ; he himself is the greatest miracle in Christianity.

We can thank God that there is a reliable apostolic witness to so stupendous a person. The apostles were truly privileged, as Christ himself pointed out: 'But blessed are your eyes for they see, and your ears for they hear; for assuredly, I say to you that many prophets and righteous men desired to see what you see, and did not see it, and to hear what you hear, and did not hear it' (Matt. 13:16-17).

To paraphrase the apostle John, 'We saw him with our eyes, we touched him with our hands and we heard his voice with our ears' (1:1-3; see also 4:14). The apostles were eyewitnesses who, for the most part, sealed their testimony to Christ with their own blood. At the Last Supper John leaned on the bosom of the Lord (John 13:23). Later John saw what happened at the crucifixion, and so he declared of himself that 'He who has seen has testified, and his testimony is true; and he knows that he is telling the truth, so that you may believe' (John 19:35). Thomas would not believe that Christ had risen from the dead until he had seen the print of the nails in Christ's hand and put his finger into the print of the nails, and put his hand into Christ's side which had been pierced by the spear (John 20:25-27).

Christ is not physically walking around on earth today. We can only know about him through the apostolic writings. That is the way God planned it — Christ prayed for those who would believe in him through the word of the apostles (John 17:20). We have not seen Christ (John 20:29; 1 Peter 1:8), but we are called upon to believe in him as we read of him in the eyewitness accounts of the apostles. Christ is declared to us (1:3); the apostles **'bear witness'** to him (1:2). People who claim to be Christians, with or without clerical garb, may speak glibly of the symbolic value of the resurrection or affirm, in the words of Peter Cameron, Australia's latest heretic, that 'God is like a house with many gates, the gates being the different religions.'[2] But the true Christian is very different — he knows that the Eternal One has become man and that the apostles have recorded their testimony to him in authoritative eyewitness accounts.

Spiritual consequences

1. Fellowship

The first consequence of believing this truth is fellowship. John writes so **'that you also may have fellowship with us; and truly our fellowship is with the Father and with his Son Jesus Christ'** (1:3). Christian fellowship is not simply enjoying oneself with other Christians at a picnic. There is nothing wrong with that, but we need to be clear first as to what constitutes Christian fellowship. Fellowship concerns sharing at the deepest level; it speaks of a partnership. It is more than friendship and, in one sense, it is more than love because we are commanded to love all, even our enemies (Matt. 5:43-48). But righteousness can have no fellowship with lawlessness nor light with darkness (2 Cor. 6:14). John says that he wants his readers to have fellowship with him (he actually says 'us') and with the Father and the Son. We can only have fellowship with someone if we ourselves are joined by saving faith to Christ and the other person also shares that same faith. Christians enjoy fellowship around the God-man Jesus Christ and the apostolic witness to him. Only those who would receive what John wrote about Christ could share in this fellowship (1:3).

Churches often go astray in this matter. In Australia during the 1960s the Presbyterian Church was involved in negotiations with the Methodist and Congregational Churches regarding a possible union — a union which actually came about in 1977 with the formation of the Uniting Church of Australia. In 1967 the General Assembly of the Presbyterian Church proposed that union be achieved first; then a commission would draw up a shared confession of faith. That is the wrong order. A Christian does not have fellowship with other professing Christians and then decide what they believe. The apostle John says that we receive the apostolic truth first, then have fellowship on that basis. Evangelical Christians cannot have fellowship with liberal 'Christians', as John Stott seems to think.[3] Evangelical Christians must seek first to be used of God to lead their liberal friends into a saving knowledge of Jesus Christ and the Word of God.

Luke tells us that the early Christians 'continued steadfastly in the apostles' doctrine and fellowship, in the breaking of bread, and in prayers' (Acts 2:42). All four things mentioned there are important, but the order is equally important. Christians may have non-Christian friends, they may enjoy their company in many respects, they may even find in certain circumstances that they are married to non-Christians,[4] but they can only have fellowship with other Christians, with those who also continue steadfastly in the apostles' doctrine. This fellowship cuts across denominations. An evangelical Presbyterian can have fellowship with a Baptist who knows the Lord, but not with a liberal Presbyterian who thinks that all religions lead to heaven. Fellowship is not based on a shared view of the form of church government, or of baptism, but on Christ and his inerrant Word.

Not only does the Christian enjoy fellowship with other Christians, but he also has fellowship with the Father and with Christ, his Son. Christians can easily fall into the trap of trying to live on a past experience. They might point back, for example, to the time when they were converted to Christ. But John emphasizes here that we are to live day by day in communion with God. We do not simply want to know *about* him; we want to know him. A man who receives a letter from an absent friend is happy, but far happier is the man who actually meets with and enjoys the immediate company of that friend.

2. *Joy*

The second consequence of believing the apostolic truth is joy: **'And these things we write to you that your joy may be full'** (1:4). Many manuscripts have *'our* joy' rather than '*your* joy' (for example, see the RSV and NIV), but either way it is clear that the Christian life is to be a life of joy (see 3 John 4). In John 15, Christ speaks of himself as the true vine while professing Christians are the branches. He tells them to abide in his love and his commandments and then adds, 'These things I have spoken to you, that my joy may remain in you, and that your joy may be full' (John 15:11).

The Christian life is a joyful life. It is a long way removed from the contrived and brainless kind of joy found in the un-controlled laughter of the so-called 'Toronto Blessing'. The Bible warns against 'the laughter of the fool' (Eccles. 7:6). Christian joy is not mere excitement, but is a calm, deep and sober happiness which is the fruit of the Holy Spirit's work in us (Gal. 5:22-23). If you profess to belong to Christ, and you find that you are constantly mournful and depressed, there is something wrong. John's first epistle was written that we might have joy. As Charles Simeon put it, 'There are but two lessons for the Christian to learn: the one is, to enjoy God in every-thing; the other is, to enjoy everything in God.'[5]

When you have fellowship with the Father, the Son and with other Christians on the basis of Christ as the Eternal One made flesh, you will know joy. You will know why you are here on earth and you will know where you are going. The world delights in a full bank account or the latest gadget for the house, but the Christian has far more reason for joy — he or she enjoys a right relationship with God and his people. So far we have seen that 1 John was written to reveal Christ to us, that we might have fellowship with God and with those who trust him too, and to experience the fulness of joy through this knowledge. These are good reasons to continue to study John's first epistle.

2.
God is light

Please read 1 John 1:5-7

God is light

Having written of fellowship and joy in Christ, John raises three false claims that have been made by the Docetists: that sin does not matter (1:6); that it is not a part of our nature (1:8) and that it is not a part of our conduct (1:10). To counter these claims, John begins by setting out the being of God, that **'God is light and in him is no darkness at all'** (1:5). Many professing evangelicals today think that the first thing we need to tell the world about God is that his very nature is love, that he loves everybody equally and that we need to respond to that love by inviting Jesus into our hearts. However soothing that might be, it is not John's message, nor is it really the message of the Bible. John's first assertion is that 'God is light'.

This assertion is not an invented message. It is not a guess, nor the product of careful research. John did not arrive at it through a diligent and strenuous use of his own intellectual powers. On the contrary, he writes that **'This is the message which we have heard from him and declare to you'** (1:5). People say, 'I like to think of God as a kindly and benevolent figure who is always there when you need him. I can leave all my problems with him.' That is not John's language. John declares, 'We apostles have heard from Christ himself what God is like, and we now declare it to you most authoritatively that God is light.'

Darkness cannot co-exist with light: **'In him is no darkness at all'** (1:5). Light shines and, because it is pure, unsullied and undiluted, it expels darkness. John is not referring here so much to light as *revealing* God but to God as the one who is utterly holy. He is so holy that evil can have no place beside him. The heavens are not pure in his sight (Job 15:15), and even the best of men, the prophet whose lips proclaimed his very Word, can only lament in his presence:

> Woe is me, for I am undone!
> Because I am a man of unclean lips,
> And I dwell in the midst of a people of unclean lips;
> For my eyes have seen the King,
> The LORD of hosts
>
>   (Isa. 6:5).

This is the God who is 'of purer eyes than to behold evil, and cannot look on wickedness' (Hab. 1:13).

It is, of course, wonderfully true that 'God is love' (1 John 4:8,16), but love is not possible without holiness (see 1 Cor. 13:4-7). If we do not grasp the holiness of God, we shall not understand what the love of God means. To many in the church today, the love of God demands that he must save all in the end, but that is not so. God's love never compromises his holiness. Well may we sing with Thomas Binney,

> Eternal Light! Eternal Light!
> How pure that soul must be,
> When, placed within thy searching sight,
> It shrinks not, but, with calm delight,
> Can live, and look on thee!

A false claim refuted

The heretics in John's day were apparently claiming to be en-joying fellowship with God, but going on in the ways of the world (1:6). They were, in effect, saying that sin does not matter. John's reply is not that Christians are perfect — not at all. The claim that we have no sin is a delusion (1:8). But John is saying that because God is holy, his people must be commit-ted to holy living. A person who claims to know God but who walks in darkness is lying and not carrying out the truth. He may believe in Jesus as Lord, he may preach and prophesy in his name, he may perform miracles and cast out demons — but if he practises lawlessness he is damned as one whom Christ never knew (Matt. 7:21-23). If we are not slaves of righteous-ness, we are slaves of sin (Rom. 6:15-18). Without holiness (or sanctification), no one will see the Lord (Heb. 12:14). The evangelist may tell the unholy believer that he is safe, but Christ says that he is not.

In John's day the Docetists with Gnostic leanings thought that the body did not come from God. This led to one of two consequences: they could turn to asceticism and torture their bodies and flagellate themselves; or they could engage in im-morality and drunkenness, or whatever, and think that their spirits were pure, so it did not matter what their bodies did. It appears that John was especially confronting the latter conse-quence. The 'Children of God' cult in the 1960s taught that people could be won to Christ through sinful means — women were even encouraged to be 'hookers for Christ'. Roman Catholics may think that they are saved because they are bap-tized and they attend mass. Professing evangelicals may ap-peal to a decision for Christ that they have made. But we are not to be deceived. Fornicators, idolaters, adulterers, homo-sexuals, sodomites, thieves, covetous people, drunkards, re-vilers and extortioners will not inherit the kingdom of God

(1 Cor. 6:9-10). In recent times the American gangster Mickey Cohen was reputedly converted, but later declared that he wanted to be a Christian gangster![1] If you find yourself habitually practising any of the works of the flesh listed in Galatians 5:19-21, you have no reason to believe that you are a Christian.

Walking in the light

If we walk in the light as God is in the light, then two results will follow. The first is that **'We have fellowship with one another'** (1:7). It is sin that mars our fellowship with God and with his people. If we are walking in the light, if we are in the kingdom of God and acting accordingly, fellowship with those who are redeemed by grace must follow. If you are not walking in the light, then your relationships with others will be affected and your prayers will be hindered (1 Peter 3:7).

The second result is that **'The blood of Jesus Christ his Son cleanses us from all sin'** (1:7). A sensitive conscience could read of what John has said about God's being light, of the possibility of our deceiving ourselves and of the need to walk in fellowship with God and one another, and become depressed. The more we contemplate the holiness of God, the more we realize that we need a God who is not only holy. We need God to be gracious too. Thank God, he is gracious; he sent his Son to shed his blood for sinners. Martin Luther once dreamt that his accuser came to him to set before him afresh all of his sins. Luther admitted them all, without denying any or seeking to justify himself in any way, but he also scrawled across the list: 'The blood of Jesus Christ cleanses us from all sin.'

Bishop Westcott made the strange suggestion that while the blood encompasses all that is involved in Christ's death, it 'always includes the thought of the life preserved and active beyond death'.[2] To put it mildly, this is strained; it is a clear reference to Christ's death on the cross. Not only does the blood of Christ secure forgiveness for the penitent sinner but cleansing too; not only is the guilt of sin atoned for but its power is broken; not only is the sinner justified but sanctified also. The believer has a new nature, a new status and a new direction. Holiness is demanded by a holy God, but holiness is also provided by him. As Thomas Binney put it:

> The sons of ignorance and night
> May dwell in the eternal Light,
> Through the eternal Love!

3.
Dealing with sin

Please read 1 John 1:8 - 2:2

In raising the subject of sin, the Bible walks a tightrope. John Stott has a valid point when he says that 'It is possible to be both too lenient and too severe towards sin.'[1] What he means is that 1 John 1:6 tells us that we cannot walk in sin and claim fellowship with God, but verses 8 and 10 tell us that we are sinners by nature and by conduct. Sin is inevitable but inexcusable — that is the terrible human dilemma. Sin breaks our fellowship with God and his people, but we cannot stop ourselves from sinning. We are commanded to be sinless, but we are bound in sin. It all seems to be too much like asking a blind man to see, a deaf man to hear, a lame man to walk, or a dead man to rise up and run. How, then, do we deal with sin?

Two false claims

We have already noted the false claim in verse 6 concerning the impossibility of walking in darkness and maintaining fellowship with God. Now we have two more false claims. The first one is found in verse 8: **'If we say that we have no sin, we deceive ourselves, and the truth is not in us.'** Many people believe that we are not born with a sinful nature, but with glorious potential. Surely, however, one of the most self-evident truths of the Christian faith is that every man, woman and child has been sinful from the day of conception. Just look around you — does not every person you know have something morally wrong with him or her? And, more importantly, look within yourself — is not sin so deeply ingrained in your heart that you are incapable of one totally righteous deed? Even in our best deeds, sin — especially the sin of pride — lurks nearby. Yet Shirley MacLaine, one of the many New Age devotees about today, came to believe, through the medium of channelling, that our souls are metaphors for God.[2] The apostle John is very blunt about such people: they are having themselves on; the truth is not in them; they give themselves away. In short, they are living in a spiritual dream world and, for all their religion, are far from Christ.

The second claim is very similar: **'If we say that we have not sinned, we make him a liar, and his word is not in us'** (1:10). It is very easy to entice people into sin. Annoy them for long enough and they become angry; feed them with falsehoods for long enough and they will believe anything; flatter them for long enough and they become proud. We are all morally fragile and vulnerable. Hence John, with his realistic view of the human condition, is again very blunt with those who claim that they have not sinned. Such people make God a liar, and his Word is not in them. God says that we have all sinned:

> The Lord looks down from heaven upon the children of
>   men,
> To see if there are any who understand, who seek God.
> They have all turned aside,
> They have together become corrupt;
> There is none who does good,
> No, not one
>
>   (Ps. 14:2-3).

'There is not a just man on earth who does good, and does not sin' (Eccles. 7:20), for 'All have sinned and fall short of the glory of God' (Rom. 3:23).

God sees us all as sinners. In 1775 Augustus Toplady (the author of 'Rock of Ages'), published an article in which he attempted to assess England's guilt as a nation in terms of a national debt. He came to the conclusion that England would never be able to pay her debt, and then calculated that if as individuals we sinned every second of our lives, we would each run up 2,522,880,000 sins by the age of eighty, if we lived that long![3] Toplady's approach has been roundly criticized but it is far closer to reality than Shirley MacLaine's rhapsodies. If we do not see ourselves as those who are utterly corrupt, if we think we are basically all right, then we are deceiving ourselves and God's truth is not in us. We would be, in reality, standing before the throne of God and calling him a liar. The person who cannot see that he is in Adam (i.e. fallen and sinful) has no reason to seek to be found in Christ (i.e. renewed and righteous). Only when we see our dreadful state before God will we ask how our sins can be taken away.

Our response to our sin

Once we have realized our terrible condition, we need to confess our sins, for God has given us a sure and certain promise: **'If we confess our sins, he is faithful and just to forgive us our sins and to cleanse us from all unrighteousness'** (1:9). The remedy is not false defence, excuse-making, blame-shifting, or a complacent shrug of the shoulders with the comment: 'Oh well, nobody's perfect.' The remedy is found in *confessing* our sins before God, for 'He who covers [or hides] his sins will not prosper, but whoever confesses and forsakes them will have mercy' (Prov. 28:13). To 'confess' is literally 'to say the same thing'; it is to agree with God against ourselves. We ought to name our sins before God, and also to anyone we have wronged. During the tragedy of Nazi Germany, Dietrich Bonhoeffer headed up a seminary of the German 'Confessing Church' at Finkenwalde. Here Bonhoeffer proclaimed, 'In confession occurs the breakthrough to the cross.'[4]

The confessing sinner is assured that God is faithful and just. God is *faithful* to his covenant promises of forgiveness: ' "Repent, and turn from all your transgressions, so that iniquity will not be your ruin. Cast away from you all the transgressions which you have committed, and get yourselves a new heart and a new spirit. For why should you die, O house of Israel? For I have no pleasure in the death of one who dies," says the Lord GOD. "Therefore turn and live!" ' (Ezek. 18:30-32). And he is *just* — which at first sight seems not much consolation. What John means is that God is just, or righteous, in punishing sinners through the death of Christ. So in forgiving sinners, God continues to be faithful and just, as Paul points out in Romans 3:25-26.

If we confess our sins, God will do two things: he will forgive us and he will cleanse us. When he *forgives* us, he cancels the huge debt that we owe to him. He wipes it out, so that we come before him as acquitted people, as if we had never sinned. Then God *cleanses* us, or purifies us (NIV); he makes the sinner holy. Because God is faithful, he forgives; because he is righteous, he cleanses. We all have need of this remedy. We are all guilty of selfishness, pride, unbelief, rash words, bad tempers, pent-up resentment and impure thoughts. Here is the remedy we need. God offers it freely to us: 'Confess your sins, and find both forgiveness and cleansing.' This is true as we begin the Christian journey by confessing our sins and believing in Christ for the first time, and also as we continue to battle with ongoing sin in our lives.

God's remedy for sin

We need a basis for our forgiveness. If the prisoner in the dock confesses his crimes, the judge does not release him on the basis of his confession. Justice must still be done; the crime must still be paid for. Otherwise, mercy will simply descend into weakness. But God has reconciled justice and mercy at the cross of Christ — and only at the cross of Christ. **'My little children, these things I write to you, that you may not sin. And if anyone sins, we have an Advocate with the Father, Jesus Christ the righteous. And he himself is the propitiation for our sins, and not for ours only but also for the whole world'** (2:1-2).

Here John is not making light of sin. We are not to say to ourselves, 'If sin is inevitable (1:8,10), why not go ahead and sin?' We are not to think that because God is merciful, he is not worried about our wrongdoing. Calvin Coolidge was President of the United States in the 1920s, and was renowned for never using an unnecessary word. One Sunday morning he went off to church, and on his return home was asked what subject the preacher had spoken about. Coolidge replied, 'Sin.' 'Well,' came the frustrated rejoinder, 'what did the preacher say about it?' Coolidge's response was characteristic: 'He was agin' it.'

God too is against sin. John writes so that we will not sin (2:1), but he has already said that we are all sinners who need to confess our sins (1:8-10). John is both a perfectionist (in that he desires perfection) and a realist (in that he knows what we human beings are like). Only those who know something of these twin motives at work in their lives can rest upon the basis that God has provided for our forgiveness. This basis is like a stool with three legs.

1. The person of Jesus Christ

John describes our Lord as **'Jesus Christ the righteous'**. We have the obligation to be righteous, but not the ability. Christ, however, is righteous, for 'In him there is no sin' (3:5). As he lay dying on 1 January 1937 J. Gresham Machen dictated a telegram to his colleague John Murray: 'I'm so thankful for active obedience of Christ. No hope without it.'[5] By this, Machen meant that he knew that his substitute is without blemish. Christ's life alone is characterized by perfect obedience to his Father's will. We cannot plead that we are righteous, for we are not, but we can plead the righteous person of Christ who fulfilled the law for us.

2. Christ's death as a propitiation

Christ is **'the propitiation for our sins'**. Many commentators shy away from the word 'propitiation'. One of the worst examples is the New English Bible, which says that Christ is 'the remedy for the defilement of our sins', a phrase that draws attention to the power, not the guilt, of sin. The RSV uses 'expiation', which at least refers to the removal of guilt. The NIV and NRSV paraphrase by referring to Christ as 'the atoning sacrifice for our sins'.

Despite the fact that it is not a word which is commonly used today, 'propitiation' conveys the right idea. John is writing of appeasing the anger of God, of satisfying his holy and perfect justice. It was the ancient pagan religions which portrayed any divine being as lacking in emotion and somewhat indifferent to holiness; not so the God of the Bible. At Calvary Christ drank until he had emptied the cup of God's righteous fury against sinners. God is slow to anger (Exod. 34:6; Neh. 9:17; Ps. 103:8) but he is angry with sin (Jer. 21:12; Ezek.

24:13; Zech. 8:16-17) and so can be said to hate sinners (Ps. 11:5-7).

Christ, however, suffered in all his sinless beauty until finally Justice cried out, 'Enough!' We can now plead the Lord Jesus Christ as our propitiation because the divine anger has already been turned away from us onto God's beloved Son. We do not propitiate God, but God, who is love (4:8,16), has propitiated himself by sending his eternal Son to satisfy his own justice. Such is the wonder of Calvary, where God's love and God's righteousness are brought together in the perfection of Christ's propitiatory sacrifice for sinners.

John says that Christ is the propitiation for the sins of the whole world. By this, he does not mean that the whole world is saved, because John knows there are two groups in the world — 'the children of God and the children of the devil' (3:10), those under the mercy of God and those under the judgement of God. When Peter on the Day of Pentecost cites the prophet Joel's promise that God would pour out his Spirit on 'all flesh' (Acts 2:17), he does not mean that everybody in the ancient world received the Spirit of God. Similarly, when John declares that Christ is the propitiation for the sins of **'the whole world'** (2:2), his main point is that Christ's propitiation includes Gentiles as well as Jews. We might add that Christ is the one and only remission for the sins of God's people down through the ages.[6] From the foundation of the world the Lamb has been slain (in the mind of God) and his people have had their names written in the Book of Life (Rev. 13:8; 17:8). But they are no tiny little group; they are 'a great multitude which no one could number of all nations, tribes, peoples, and tongues' (Rev. 7:9).

3. Christ is the sinner's Advocate

The Greek word translated 'Advocate' is often anglicized as 'Paraclete'. Christ is our Paraclete and in John 14:16 the Holy

Spirit is described as 'another Paraclete'. The word has been translated as 'Comforter' and 'Helper', but 'Legal Defender' gives the right idea. If I have an advocate in a human court of law, I expect him to dwell on my good points. If he wanted to list all my sins to the judge, I would soon want another advocate. But that is not how Christ pleads for his elect. Christ died for his elect and he makes intercession for them (Rom. 8:33-34). But what is he saying to his Father? He is certainly not listing our good points as a human advocate would. He does not plead the sinner's innocence, for that would be a lie (see 1:8,10). Instead, he pleads his sacrifice, for that is sufficient.

We are sinners by nature (what we are) and by conduct (what we do). If we cannot see that, we have not taken the first step in understanding the gospel. Even if we are convicted at this point, we still have a problem. God's remedy is that we must confess our sins on the basis of Christ's righteous character, his propitiatory death and his advocacy of his people before the throne of God. We are not cured just because we realize we are sick — that is only the start of the cure. We must apply God's remedy for sinners, as Charles Wesley did:

> Arise, my soul, arise,
> Shake off thy guilty fears;
> The bleeding Sacrifice
> In my behalf appears:
> Before the throne my Surety stands,
> My name is written on his hands.

4.
Two tests

Please read 1 John 2:3-11

1 John is an epistle about assurance. How can we know who is a Christian? How can you know that you are a Christian? Robert Murray M'Cheyne used to advise, 'For every look at self, take ten looks at Christ!' That is still the best place to start, for Christ must be both our justification and our sanctification (1 Cor. 1:30). Nevertheless, while avoiding an unhealthy introspection, we still need to heed the apostolic word to 'Examine yourselves as to whether you are in the faith' (2 Cor. 13:5). In 1 John 2:3-11, John proposes two tests for the professing Christian. The first one is the moral test of obedience and the second one is the social test of love. These two criteria do not exhaust what the Bible says about testing ourselves, but they form two crucial tests for us all.

The test of obedience

John writes simply, **'Now by this we know** [present tense] **that we know** [perfect tense, conveying the sense that a past action has results that continue into the present] **him, if we keep his commandments'** (2:3) Assurance comes partly through keeping God's commandments. As Jesus said, 'If you love me, keep my commandments' (John 14:15). What happens when the believer falls into sin? He loses his firm conviction that he belongs to God. After David committed adultery with Bathsheba and virtually murdered her husband Uriah, he was forgiven when he confessed his sin to Nathan the prophet (2 Sam. 12:13), but he did not have much peace for a time. Hence he prayed,

> Do not cast me away from your presence,
> And do not take your Holy Spirit from me.
> Restore to me the joy of your salvation
>
> (Ps. 51:11-12).

Assurance is not something we receive simply by saying we believe in Jesus. A growing obedience will lead to a humble, yet growing assurance.

We should be clear that John is not saying that only those who are morally perfect can know that they are Christians. He has already made it clear that those who think they have reached perfection are deceiving themselves, making God a liar and showing that his word of truth is not in them (1:8,10). Rather, he is describing those who, in Calvin's words, 'strive, according to the capacity of human infirmity, to form their life in conformity to the will of God.'[1] It is the message of Psalm 119: 'Make me walk in the path of your commandments, for I delight in it' (v. 35); 'I love your commandments more than gold, yes, than fine gold!' (v. 127); 'Direct my steps by your word, and let no iniquity have dominion over me' (v. 133); 'Your law is my delight' (v. 174). That is not the delusion of any claim to sinless perfection, but the delight of a redeemed sinner in seeking to obey God's revealed Word.

Nor is John describing the way of salvation. He is not saying, 'If you obey God's law, God will take you to heaven.' John is describing one of the characteristics of a true Christian, not setting out how to become a Christian. Those who

have confessed their sins (1:9) on the basis of Christ's righteous propitiation (2:1-2) need to test that profession by the
evidence of a growing obedience to God's law. It is a case of,
as Luther told Zwingli in 1529, 'If Scripture commanded me
to eat dung, I would do so.'

John is very clear on this: **'He who says, "I know him,"
and does not keep his commandments, is a liar, and the
truth is not in him'** (2:4). Many professing evangelicals today teach that 'No Christian is under the law as a rule of life.'
The so-called lordship controversy has seen professing
evangelicals maintain that, to be saved, Christians need only
believe in Jesus as Saviour. Bowing to him as Lord can be left
to a second and optional work of grace. In responding to this
teaching, Ernest Reisinger cites one *Handbook of Personal
Evangelism* from Florida Bible College which declares that
'Any teaching that demands a change of conduct toward either
God or man for salvation is to add works or human effort to
faith, and this contradicts all scripture and is an accursed message.'[2] This is a God-dishonouring and dangerous error. While
it is true that we cannot be saved by works, it is also true that
without holiness (or sanctification) we shall not see the Lord
(Heb. 12:14). The Spirit-filled Christian is the law-filled Christian; he has the law of God written upon his heart (Jer. 31:33;
Ezek. 36:27). He does not sing,

> I'm saved by grace, oh, happy condition!
> I can transgress every day and still claim remission.

The person who is indifferent to God's law but complacently
says, 'I believe in Jesus,' is deceiving himself and others.

Love and law are not contradictory, for **'Whoever keeps
his word, truly the love of God is perfected in him. By this
we know that we are in him'** (2:5). The writer Jan Morris
speaks for many today when she says that 'The Ten Commandments are malicious. They are much too precise. Precision

is the worst thing of all... There's only one Commandment that's really necessary, "Be Kind". St Paul got it right when he said the greatest of the fruits of the spirit is charity.'[3] Error can be very beguiling — hence the need for John to write his epistle. The Bible makes no such dichotomy between love and law. By our obeying God's Word, his love is 'perfected', or 'made mature', or 'made complete', in us. John almost certainly has in mind our love for God rather than God's love for us.

George G. Findlay has some helpful things to say here, especially in these permissive days. He points out that 'Obedience is the school of love's perfecting. For love's sake we obey rule, and by obeying learn to love better. Love reaches no height of perfectness in any family without commands to keep and tasks to do; where all is ease and indulgence, selfishness grows rank. There is a kind of strictness fatal to love; but there is another kind, which is its guardian and nurse. The most orderly households are, in general, the most affectionate, while the ill-governed teem with bickering and spite.'[4] The Christian life is to be one of maturing in obedience and love.

Through our obedience to the Word of God, our love for him matures and develops. This does not take place overnight. When the immature and awkward Charles Simeon first visited the home of Henry Venn, the three Venn daughters could only laugh at his looks and manners. Henry Venn decided to teach them a lesson. He took them out into the garden and told them to bring him a peach. As it was still early summer, they had to make do with an unripe one. 'Well, my dears, it is green now,' said the kindly old man, 'and we must wait; but a little more sun and a few more showers, and the peach will be ripe and sweet. So it is with Mr Simeon.'[5] In this life we are to mature; perfection will come when Christ returns and we are made like him, for we shall see him as he is (3:2). This growth in love for God and in obedience to him leads also to a growth in assurance that he is ours and we are his.

John fleshes out what he means in verse 6: **'He who says he abides in him ought himself also to walk just as he walked.'** John was not always very particular with his pronouns. When he refers to 'he' or 'him', he can often mean the Father or the Son, but in verse 6 he is obviously referring to the Lord Jesus Christ. One commentator — Kenneth Grayston — thinks that the Epistle of John was written as a 'trial run' for the Gospel of John.[6] That seems unlikely. Certainly, John expected his readers to have quite an extensive knowledge of the life and ministry of their Lord and Saviour, as set out, for example, in the Gospel of John. Hence John could tell his first-century readers, and also us, to imitate Christ.

John's opponents denied the full humanity of Christ, so they could not imitate him (4:2; 2 John 7). Yet they claimed to abide or remain in Christ.[7] One of the evidences that we are savingly united to Christ is that we will 'walk' as he walked. This means that our lifestyle will be one which is habitually and consistently based upon that of the Lord Jesus Christ. Clearly, we cannot imitate our Lord in his deity — in forgiving sinners as he did (cf. Mark 2:1-12), or raising the dead (e.g. John 11) or judging the world (e.g. John 5:28-29). But we are to imitate his goodness, his meekness, his self-sacrifice, his love and his submission to the Father. This is to walk as Christ walked, and it is one of the proofs that we are indeed Christians.

The test of obedience thus has two prongs — obeying God's commandments and imitating Christ. If these strike a chord in your heart, you can be sure that that is because God the Holy Spirit is working in you.

The test of love

The second test of the Christian's profession is love: **'Brethren [actually, "Beloved"], I write no new commandment to**

you, but an old commandment which you have had from the beginning. The old commandment is the word which you heard from the beginning. Again, a new commandment I write to you, which thing is true in him and in you, because the darkness is passing away, and the true light is already shining' (2:7-8). Robert Candlish contended that the new commandment was the word of life, not the command to love one's Christian brother.[8] But John is surely referring back to Jesus' words in John 13:34: 'A new commandment I give to you, that you love one another; as I have loved you, that you also love one another.' This commandment is both old and new. It is there in the Old Testament: 'You shall love your neighbour as yourself' (Lev. 19:18). But in the New Testament Christ gives it new meaning, power and impetus.

Francis Schaeffer had every reason to refer to love as 'the mark of the Christian'.[9] The apostle John is no less blunt: **'He who says he is in the light, and hates his brother, is in darkness until now'** (2:9). **'But he who hates his brother is in darkness and walks in darkness, and does not know where he is going, because the darkness has blinded his eyes'** (2:11). If we have the Spirit, we are Christians (Rom. 8:9). This will also mean that we have the ninefold fruit of the Spirit, which is headed by love (Gal. 5:22-23). A person without the Spirit is in darkness. When we hate, we are in darkness. When we are in darkness — which is our natural condition (John 8:12; Eph. 4:17-18) — our vision is distorted, and it is easy to see things that are not there. A person full of hate is prickly, and his hate preys upon his imagination. He takes offence at the smallest things, and maintains a long memory and an unforgiving spirit. No matter what his profession, a person who is paralysed with bitterness and resentment has no reason to believe that he belongs to Christ. So much professed love today is nothing more than disguised selfishness — the aim is not the holy welfare of the other person but the satisfaction of one's own wants. 'I love you' can easily mean 'I love me and I want you to gratify me.'

The heretics made a number of claims: to have fellowship with God (1:6), to be without sin (1:8,10), to know God (2:4), to abide in Christ (2:6), to be in the light (2:9) and to love God (4:20). In 1:5-7 'walking in darkness' refers to 'walking in sin', but in 2:8-11 it refers to hating one's brother. For the counterfeit Christian, **'The darkness has blinded his eyes'** (2:11); for the true Christian **'The true light is already shining'** (2:8). If the true light is shining in us, that will be expressed in terms of love and compassion towards our fellow believers. To cite Horatius Bonar:

> Beloved, let us love:
> In love is light,
> And he who loveth not,
> Dwelleth in night.

To fail to love is to show that we dwell in darkness, apart from God who is both light and love.

John writes, **'He who loves his brother abides in the light, and there is no cause for stumbling in him'** (2:10). There are two interrelated principles at work here. To cite Candlish: 'Being in the light begets brotherly love, and brotherly love secures abiding in the light.'[10] As for the identity of the one in whom there is no cause for stumbling, that is not immediately obvious. The Good News Bible translates the passage to say that the loving Christian will not cause another to stumble. This truth is taught in Romans 14:14-15: 'I know and am convinced by the Lord Jesus that there is nothing unclean of itself; but to him who considers anything to be unclean, to him it is unclean. Yet if your brother is grieved because of your food, you are no longer walking in love. Do not destroy with your food the one for whom Christ died.' However, the New International Version understands that the loving Christian himself (or herself) will not stumble. Sometimes John seems to be deliberately ambiguous. That is probably not true here, for John's focus is centred on the reader, not the brother. Therefore, the interpretation of the NIV would appear more likely than that of the GNB. Yet, for all that, both interpretations make good sense. Loving others will mean that we will not cause them offence and we will ourselves be upheld in love.

How about our lives? Do we readily submit to God's Word in our lives, in the way we interact with our families, the world and the church? Do we love other Christians, or are our lives characterized by selfishness, indifference, pettiness and pent-up resentment? Is our faith in Christ a true faith? The false believer will give himself away: 'Yes, I feel good,' or 'Yes, I have been baptized,' or 'Yes, I try to be kind to others.' Grace is received by faith and leads to works (Eph. 2:8-10). Do you find within yourself a Spirit-inspired desire to obey God's Word, imitate Christ and love his people?

5.
The Christian and the world

Please read 1 John 2:12-17

There is no greater temptation for Christians than that of drawing a very fuzzy line between the church and the world — or even no line at all! In some parts of the Western world this has become so serious that there are even homosexual churches. Hence John addresses various members of the congregation, and then warns them to beware of the world. Christian love is never indiscriminate — it makes no sense, for example, to profess love for God and for the devil. Those who love the Lord hate evil (Ps. 97:10; Rom. 12:9).

Addressing various groups in the church

Here John addresses three groups within the church — little children, fathers and young men. He may be referring to chronological age or to spiritual maturity. In verse 1 of the same chapter 'little children' is used to describe all Christians, so it is possible that in verses 12-14 John is referring to all Christians, then the leaders (the fathers) and the future leaders (the young men).[1] This would explain why there is no explicit reference to women.[2] However, this would seem to be a rather confusing way to address the congregation, and it is more likely that John is writing to the three groups in terms of their spiritual development.

1 John is an epistle about testing and reassuring Christians. Here, in chapter 2:12-14, John is reassuring his readers. John addresses the children as forgiven and as having known the Father; the fathers as having known him who is from the beginning ('he' can be either the Father or the Son, but is more likely to refer to the Son); and the young men as having overcome the wicked one and as being those in whom the Word of God abides, bringing strength.

All these descriptions when pulled together give a good definition of a Christian: he is forgiven for Christ's sake; he knows Christ; in Christ he has overcome Satan; and he is strong in the abiding Word of God. It is instructive that many of the key verbs in verses 12-14 are in the perfect tense. This tense is used when an action in the past has effects which continue on into the present. Therefore, from the time of his conversion onwards, the Christian knows abiding forgiveness through Christ. He also knows — and continues to know — the eternal Christ and the eternal Father. Christ's victory over Satan means that the Christian enjoys the abiding consequences of that victory in the present. John is here not so much referring to ongoing victories over Satan's temptations but to the once-for-all victory at conversion. At his conversion the sinner was moved to repent and put his faith in Christ alone, and so was removed from the dominion of Satan to that of Christ. At the cross the ruler of this world was cast out (John 12:31), and Christ made a public spectacle of principalities and powers in disarming them (Col. 2:15). This victory of Christ in the past is then owned by the Christian in the present.

This makes the believer strong and the word of God abides[3] or remains in him (see 2:14). Here John switches to the present tense. The victory gained over the evil one at conversion is to be experienced in spiritual strength which enables the Christian to overcome temptations in day-to-day life. As with Christ himself in his own temptations (Matt. 4:1-11), it is the Word of God which enables the Christian to fight successfully against the wiles of the devil (see also Eph. 6:10-17). These things together characterize the Christian, so it is good for the reader to ask himself or herself, 'Do they characterize me?'

Note too the varied groups in the church. The church is a covenant community comprised of all kinds of people, of differing ages and varying levels of spiritual maturity. The youth group is not the covenant community, nor is the women's group, the Sunday School, the university Christian Union, or the men's fellowship. God's people are not restricted to any one age-group. In the Old Testament God commanded that his law be read every seven years to all Israel: 'Gather the people together, men and women and little ones, and the stranger who is within your gates, that they may hear and that they may learn to fear the Lord your God and carefully observe all the words of this law, and that their children, who have not known it, may hear and learn to fear the LORD your God as long as you live in the land which you cross the Jordan to possess' (Deut. 31:12-13; see also Neh. 8:2) Nor are God's people restricted to any one spiritual age-group. We ought to be maturing in the faith (Eph. 4:13-15), but it is, alas, all too true that Christians can believe and behave like babes in Christ (as, for example, in 1 Cor. 3:1 and Heb. 5:12-14).

Not loving the world

John gives us an unmistakable warning: **'Do not love the world or the things in the world. If anyone loves the world, the love of the Father is not in him'** (2:15). Whatever could John mean? Does not God love the world? (John 3:16). Are we to despise nature, when Christ himself declared that not even Solomon in all his glory was arrayed as the lilies of the field? (Matt. 6:28-29). Are we to pit ourselves against all humanity, when Christ told us to love our enemies? (Matt. 5:44-45). Clearly, John means us to form no deep attachment to the world which is in rebellion against God. We are to have no intimate fellowship with the world, nor are we to participate in a worldly lifestyle.

Our Lord told his disciples, 'If the world hates you, you know that it hated me before it hated you. If you were of the world, the world would love its own. Yet because you are not of the world, but I chose you out of the world, therefore the world hates you' (John 15:18-19). Paul commands us not to be conformed to this world. As J. B. Phillips puts it, 'Don't let the world around you squeeze you into its own mould' (Rom. 12:2). James is no less blunt: 'Friendship with the world is enmity with God.' In fact, 'Whoever ... wants to be a friend of the world makes himself an enemy of God' (James 4:4).

There is a right way and a wrong way to love the world. If your deepest attachment is to this life — this fallen world with its values — then you will make no sense of the Christian message to die to self and follow Christ. Things need to be loved in their right proportion. Money is most useful, but the love of money is a root of all kinds of evil (1 Tim. 6:10); clothes are fine, but too deep an attachment to the whims of fashion is not; sport can be healthy, but too ardent a devotion to it is spiritually unhealthy; work is a necessary thing, but man cannot live by work alone. We are not to set our hearts on this world.

Reasons for not loving the world

Why not love the world? John gives us two very cogent reasons.

1. We cannot serve two masters

'**Do not love the world or the things in the world. If anyone loves the world, the love of the Father is not in him.
For all that is in the world — the lust of the flesh, the lust
of the eyes, and the pride of life — is not of the Father but
is of the world**' (2:15-16). Either we are motivated by love
for the Father or love for the world. As Augustine puts it,
'The good make use of this world in order to enjoy God,
whereas the evil want to make use of God in order to enjoy
the world.'[4]

The lust of the flesh, the lust of the eyes and the pride of life
all indicate a wrong love of the world. Eve ate of the tree of
the knowledge of good and evil because she 'saw that the tree
was good for food, that it was pleasant to the eyes, and a tree
desirable to make one wise' (Gen. 3:6). Achan coveted a
Babylonian garment, 200 shekels of silver and a wedge of gold
at Jericho, and so aroused the wrath of God (Josh. 7:1,20-
21). David sinned when he lusted after Bathsheba before he
actually committed adultery with her (2 Sam. 11:2-3; Matt.
5:28). These are just three examples of what it means to give
in to the lust of the flesh, the lust of the eyes and the pride of
life. Keep 1 John 2:16 open when the advertisers are appeal-
ing to you. These three motivations are usually there — the
car is flashy; the perfume or the after-shave is alluring; the
new set of clothes will cause you to exude sex-appeal and an
aura of success. In fact, our pride can mean that even great
acts of charity may be of the world.

The Christian is to resist all this. The world is beautiful in
some respects, but in other respects it is a sham. The Christian
does not sing naïvely, 'What a wonderful world!' for in its
fallen state the world is anything but wonderful. It is Vanity
Fair. People hide behind masks, play games and avoid reality.
Glitter is not substance, sentimentality is not true affection,
glamour is not the same as beauty and laughter is no proof of

joy within. To cite John Henry Newman, 'The world is sweet to the lips, but bitter to the taste. It pleases at first, but not at last. It looks gay on the outside, but evil and misery lie concealed within.'⁵ Your heart belongs either to God or to the world, and these two masters are mutually incompatible.

2. *The world is only temporary*

The second reason for not giving your heart to the world is that this world is only temporary: **'And the world is passing away, and the lust of it; but he who does the will of God abides for ever'** (2:17). Beauty fades away after a few decades at the most; wealth is uncertain; fame is short-lived; popularity is always precarious. It is not just the failures in life that disappoint us, for even the successes can never fully satisfy. Our age is dominated by pop music, show business, fashion and sport — sure signs of its decay. We come into this world with nothing and we shall leave it with nothing (1 Tim. 6:7; see also 1 Cor. 7:31). That provides us with a Christian perspective. Why put your money on a world that is perishing? You would not buy a car if you knew it would fall apart in two weeks. Why, then, give your heart to something that will not last? 'For the things which are seen are temporary, but the things which are not seen are eternal' (2 Cor. 4:18). This world is, as Bunyan said, 'the City of Destruction'.

We have a promise of something far better: 'He who does the will of God abides for ever.' This is something that is sure and eternal, which cannot fade, rust or fall apart. So John Cennick urges us to sing,

Lift your eyes, you sons of light;
Zion's city is in sight;
There our endless home shall be,
There our Lord we soon shall see.

The Christian is on his way to a palace; to become attached to a broken-down cottage would be absurd. The Christian seeks a prize of gold; to be sidetracked by lumps of dirt would be folly. The apostle Peter wrote to Christians as 'sojourners and pilgrims' (1 Peter 2:11). If you are such, you cannot be waylaid by the lust of the flesh, the lust of the eyes and the pride (what G. G. Findlay called the 'vainglory') of life. You have every reason to seek God and no good reason to embrace this transient and unsatisfying world.

6.
Beware of antichrists!

Please read 1 John 2:18-27

To many people today, to be a Christian means to be tolerant of just about any belief. Such people see disputes over doctrine as inherently unchristian. What they desire in the church is peace and unity. But, as we have seen, the apostle John sets out three tests for the Christian — right doctrine, a right attitude to others and a right view of God's law. All three tests go together. In 1 John 2:18-27 John concentrates on the battle between a true and a false view of Christ. The reader will recall that John has already laid the foundation for dealing with this topic in the opening verses of his epistle (1:1-4).

A warning about antichrists

The apostles managed to convey severe warnings with tender affection: **'Little children, it is the last hour; and as you have heard that the Antichrist is coming, even now many antichrists have come, by which we know that it is the last hour'** (2:18). The Old Testament looked forward to 'that day' or 'the latter days' when God would act decisively to judge evil and redeem his people (e.g. Amos 8:9-11; 9:9-12; Isa. 2). In the New Testament we find that this takes place in two stages — the victory is achieved in principle at Calvary and

will be consummated when Jesus comes again and every knee
will bow and every tongue confess that he is Lord. Hence, the
expressions 'the last hour', 'the last times', or 'the last days'
refer to any time between the resurrection of the Lord Jesus
Christ and his glorious coming again (see, for example, Acts
2:17; Heb. 1:1-2; 1 Peter 1:20). They do not, as such, refer to
the last decade or so before Christ comes again, as so many
today believe.

Before Christ comes, the Antichrist will come, as the apostle
Paul told us: 'Let no one deceive you by any means; for that
Day will not come unless the falling away comes first, and the
man of sin is revealed, the son of perdition, who opposes and
exalts himself above all that is called God or that is worshipped,
so that he sits as God in the temple of God, showing himself
that he is God... The coming of the lawless one is according to
the working of Satan, with all power, signs, and lying wonders' (2 Thess. 2:3-4,9). From the New Testament's perspective, the coming Antichrist is a religious figure — as opposed
to a brutal secular figure such as Hitler or Stalin. Yet even in
the first century there were many antichrists. Whatever we
make of *the* Antichrist — and the *Westminster Confession of
Faith* identifies him with the papacy — it is undeniable that
there must be antichrists today.

The Greek word *'anti'* can mean 'against' or 'in place of'.
It is the second meaning which fits better in this context. An
antichrist is a religious teacher who proclaims a Christ who is
not the Christ of the Bible. He may be a Christ who is not
quite God and never quite saves (as the cults teach), a Christ
who offers health and wealth (as proclaimed by many television evangelists), a Christ who is repeatedly sacrificed in the
mass (as Roman Catholicism teaches), or a Christ whom you
invite into your life to make you feel good (as so much of
modern evangelicalism teaches). For all their variations, these
are the teachings of religious antichrists. We need to beware
of them.

In John's day there had been a group which had left the church to proclaim a different Christ: **'They went out from us, but they were not of us; for if they had been of us, they would have continued with us; but they went out that they might be made manifest, that none of them were of us'** (2:19). A true Christian will always persevere to the end. Jesus has promised the sheep for whom he, as the Good Shepherd, died, 'I give them eternal life, and they shall never perish; neither shall anyone snatch them out of my hand' (John 10:28). Those who leave the true people of God to embrace another Christ were never Christians in the first place.

One fateful Sunday in May 1941 on the island of Tanna in the New Hebrides (now called Vanuatu) Presbyterian missionaries went to their churches to preach and found that hardly anyone had turned up to worship God. There was a widespread apostasy — which devastated the Roman Catholics and Seventh Day Adventists as well — to the John Frum Cargo cult. This cult repudiated any contact with Europeans, and called for a return to traditional pagan customs of polygamy, dancing and kava drinking. John was supposed to be coming from America with all the cargo required for an earthly paradise. Such a sudden apostasy reveals that something drastic was wrong with the professed conversions of those who had previously claimed to be Christians.

There is a battle not just between love and hatred, or holiness and sin, but between truth and error. There were antichrists, and there are antichrists, who seek to lead people away from the true Christ.

Tests of true Christianity

It is probably fair to say that many people hear a teacher and say to themselves, 'This person is a nice person. I will believe what he says.' That is a most dangerous method. In this section of Scripture, John sets out for us three methods of discerning truth about Christ.

1. Profession concerning Jesus Christ

The first test is the profession concerning Jesus Christ: **'Who is a** [literally, "the"] **liar but he who denies that Jesus is the Christ? He is antichrist who denies the Father and the Son. Whoever denies the Son does not have the Father either; he who acknowledges the Son has the Father also'** (2:22-23). The false teachers whom John had in mind were certain Gnostics who believed that the divine Christ had descended on the man Jesus at his baptism, then left him before the crucifixion. Hence there was no real incarnation — Jesus Christ is not trusted as one person in two natures, human and divine.

John is teaching that the God-man Jesus Christ is the one and only way to the Father; he alone reveals the Father to us (Matt. 11:27; John 1:18; 14:9). This condemns Freemasonry, which teaches its adherents to call upon God without mentioning the name of Christ. It condemns prayers at inter-faith services where the name of Christ is omitted for fear that it might cause offence. It condemns the New Age movement, which uses Christian terms and even speaks of Christ. But when the New Ager speaks of being born again, he does not mean that the Holy Spirit has come upon a sinner and given that person a new disposition to seek after God. What the New Ager means is that the person lets go of himself and allows his higher self to take control. Similarly when New Agers speak of Christ, they mean the divine Christ that they claim descended on Buddha, Mohammed, Jesus and many others. 'Father' Matthew Fox (once a Roman Catholic priest, now an Episcopalian priest) says that 'Jesus is not the exclusive way' and that 'Mother Earth is Jesus Christ crucified today.' It is not enough for people to acknowledge certain Christian expressions while discarding the Bible's clear teaching that the man Jesus is the divine Christ, and is the only mediator between God and sinful human beings. An antichrist rejects the Son and so rejects the Father also.

2. *Testimony of the Spirit*

The second test concerns the testimony of the Holy Spirit. John is writing to Christians, and Christians have the Spirit of God indwelling them: **'But you have an anointing from the Holy One, and you know all things. I have not written to you because you do not know the truth, but because you know it, and that no lie is of the truth'** (2:20-21). Some commentators think that this anointing is God's Word, but it is much more likely to be the Spirit whom Jesus promised: 'And I will pray the Father, and he will give you another Helper, that he may abide with you for ever — the Spirit of truth, whom the world cannot receive, because it neither sees him nor knows him; but you know him, for he dwells with you and will be in you' (John 14:16-17). Paul takes this up in 2 Corinthians: 'Now he who establishes us with you in Christ and has anointed us is God, who also has sealed us and given us the Spirit in our hearts as a guarantee' (2 Cor. 1:21-22). As Jesus was anointed with the Spirit, so too Christians are anointed with him.

Because of the Spirit's indwelling them, Christians 'know all things' (2:20; NKJV; so too the NRSV). Or perhaps, as the RSV and NIV have it, all Christians know the truth. Whatever the case, the NKJV's rendering of verse 20 fits in with the meaning of verse 27: **'But the anointing which you have received from him abides in you, and you do not need that anyone teach you; but as the same anointing teaches you concerning all things, and is true, and is not a lie, and just as it has taught you, you will abide in him.'** John is not abolishing human teachers; the New Testament church has a decided place for them (see Eph. 4:11; 1 Tim. 3:2). After all, even John himself wrote this epistle to teach his readers! What he is saying is that the real teacher is the Holy Spirit. The Holy Spirit indwells the Christian as a kind of divine lie detector.

In the days of wicked King Ahab of Israel, Jehoshaphat, the godly King of Judah, listened to 400 'prophets' who spoke in the name of the Lord and declared that Israel and Judah should combine to defeat Syria at Ramoth Gilead. But Jehoshaphat remained suspicious that this was not right, so he asked again, 'Is there not still a prophet of the LORD here, that we may enquire of him?' (2 Chron. 18:6). The Spirit had given Jehoshaphat a love of the truth and a measure of discernment. In the New Testament he has come in an even greater way to protect his people from error and lead them in the way of truth.

Without the Spirit, people will believe in a Christ of their own imagination, one who fits in with their own whims. With the Spirit, the Christian will discern all things — not exhaustively, of course, but comprehensively. The Christian may be duped for a time, but he will hear alarm bells when someone says, 'What matters is that we all believe in God and that we have a unity of the Spirit — those are the main things.' The Christian senses that such sentiments are inadequate and ambiguous and will finally reject them. Without the Spirit, we shall be blown about by every wind of doctrine and the latest fad on the church scene. That is why it is impossible to get through to a person without the Spirit of God. Such a person does not understand, and cannot understand, the things of God (1 Cor. 2:14).

3. Holding onto apostolic teaching

The third test is found in verse 24: **'Therefore let that abide in you which you heard from the beginning. If what you**

heard from the beginning abides in you, you also will abide in the Son and in the Father.' Christians aim to believe and teach what the apostles believed and taught. There is no warrant for novelties, fashions and additions which tickle itching ears. Christianity cannot be updated to make it relevant; all that needs to be done is that it be applied faithfully. As Paul came towards the end of his life, he wrote to young Timothy, 'Hold fast the pattern of sound words which you have heard from me, in faith and love which are in Christ Jesus' (2 Tim. 1:13). Paul was certainly not encouraging Timothy to be innovative and creative in his beliefs, but to stick to 'the old, old story' of Jesus and his love.

Back in the nineteenth century Charles Hodge boasted of Princeton Seminary: 'I am not afraid to say that a new idea never originated in this seminary.'[1] That might have been expressed less baldly, but it does emphasize the need to remain faithful to the apostolic word. Neglect this word, and you are a sitting duck for any sort of teaching — religious or irreligious. That is why we must test all teaching by the light of God's inerrant and sufficient Word (Acts 17:11).

John wrote as he did because there are people who are deceiving themselves and who wish to deceive others: **'These things I have written to you concerning those who try to deceive you'** (2:26). There are teachers who profess to be Christians but who are not. They may have their own television 'ministries', but all is not as it appears on the surface. Our Lord himself warned us: 'For false christs and false prophets will rise and show signs and wonders to deceive, if possible, even the elect' (Mark 13:22). We need to beware, for these men and women will not have 'false teacher' neatly inscribed on their foreheads. That is why Christ tells us to take heed, for we need to be told about these things beforehand (Mark 13:23). The Christian life is not all straightforward; it is not all plain sailing. We need to test all things that we hear from teachers

(1 Thess. 5:21). We can do this by testing their profession of Jesus as the Messiah and God's only begotten Son, by the inward testimony of the Holy Spirit in us and by the faithfulness of these teachers to the apostolic word of Scripture.

This is not to be nit-picking and uncooperative; this is to exercise Christian discernment. Those who swallow everything will take in spiritual poison. Deceivers will not necessarily attack the faith openly, but they are still antichrists. Beware of them; know that the truth is of Jesus Christ, witnessed to by his Word and his Spirit. It is a fallen and dangerous world that we live in, and we need to be armed.

> Soldiers of Christ, arise!
> And put your armour on,
> Strong in the strength which God supplies
> Through his eternal Son.
>
> (Charles Wesley)

7.
Living in God's family

Please read 1 John 2:28 - 3:3

We have all looked at a child and said, 'Oh, yes, doesn't he look like his father?' or 'She looks exactly like her great-aunt.' We say that because there is a family likeness. In God's family too there is a family likeness. The Bible teaches that every Christian has been adopted into God's family: 'You received the Spirit of adoption by whom we cry out, "Abba, Father." The Spirit himself bears witness with our spirit that we are children of God, and if children, then heirs' (Rom. 8:15-17; see John 1:12-13; Gal. 4:4-7). When the Holy Spirit comes upon a sinner, he causes that person to trust in Christ alone for salvation, and then he or she is adopted into God's family. Many people today think that Jesus came to teach us that we are all God's children, but it is not so. We *become* God's children and are able to call upon our Father in heaven only after we have cast ourselves upon God's grace in Christ. But having become God's children, we must then grow in the family likeness and in the hope that God has given to his children.

Two foundational truths

John tells us about what it means to be a part of God's family, but he makes two foundational truths very clear for us.

1. God is righteous

'If you know that he is righteous, you know that everyone who practises righteousness is born of him' (2:29). The 'he' in verse 28 refers to Christ, but John seems to change the subject very abruptly to God in verse 29, or at least in the second half of the verse. To understand the love of God, we need to tie it in with the righteousness of God.

> For the Lord is righteous,
> He loves righteousness;
> His countenance beholds the upright
>
> (Ps: 11:7).

God is totally righteous, pure and good, without any trace of sin. He is not full of vague benevolence but of holy righteousness, devoted to the good and hating what is evil.

2. Christ is coming again

'And now, little children, abide in him, that when he appears, we may have confidence and not be ashamed before him at his coming' (2:28). Also, **'Beloved, now we are children of God; and it has not yet been revealed what we shall be, but we know that when he is revealed, we shall be like him, for we shall see him as he is'** (3:2). This is the Christian hope — that this world is not all there is, but that Christ will come again, raise the dead, judge the whole world and gather his people to himself to be with him for ever. James Montgomery Boice says that the return of Christ is mentioned 318 times in the 260 chapters of the New Testament.[1] Yet so often we carry on as if it hardly rated a mention!

The righteous King has come once; the righteous King will come again. Take away these truths, and the Bible makes no sense. That is why only a person who believes Christian doctrine has any incentive to obey Christian ethics. People shake their heads and say, 'I cannot understand what the world is coming to,' or 'It baffles me why my children are so rebellious.' Part of the answer is that a person who is not a Christian has no reason to behave like a Christian.

The response of the child of God to these truths

There are three parts to the response of the child of God to these truths.

1. The Christian will practise righteousness

'If you know that he is righteous, you know that everyone who practises righteousness is born of him' (2:29). You see how logical it all is? Since God is righteous, his children will practise righteousness. Candlish has a timely warning against any complacent misunderstanding of this notion: ' "He can't be wrong whose life is in the right," is a perilous half-truth.'[2] Virtually all truths can be distorted and misused. Nevertheless, John is saying that it is a case of 'Like father, like son'. If we are Christians — that is, if we have been born again of the Spirit of God — we will habitually act in a righteous way. That is one of the proofs that we are born of God.

Such a lifestyle will give us confidence as we think on Christ's coming again (2:28). Some will be ashamed at Christ's coming. They will be ashamed of their disordered lives, of the time they wasted watching rubbish on television, of their infidelity to their marriage partners, of their indifference to their children, of their seeking after the pleasures of this world and of their scoffing at the idea that God will judge us all. What terrible shame they will experience! The book of Revelation gives us an inkling of what it will be like: 'And the kings of the earth, the great men, the rich men, the commanders, the mighty men, every slave and every free man, hid themselves in the caves and in the rocks of the mountains, and said to the mountains and rocks, "Fall on us and hide us from the face of him who sits on the throne and from the wrath of the Lamb! For the great day of his wrath has come, and who is able to stand?" ' (Rev. 6:15-17). It is the worst kind of irony — the unbeliever faces the wrath of the *Lamb,* of the one who was sacrificed for sinners. The sinner faces the horror of wrath when he could have enjoyed the delights of mercy. That is the deepest kind of shame.

The Christian, on the other hand, views Christ's second coming as a spur to holy living: **'And everyone who has this hope in him purifies himself, just as he is pure'** (3:3). What we believe affects how we live. It is true that Christ's second coming is a doctrine of unspeakable comfort to Christians: 'Let not your heart be troubled; you believe in God, believe also in me. In my Father's house are many mansions; if it were not so, I would have told you. I go to prepare a place for you. And if I go and prepare a place for you, I will come again and receive you to myself; that where I am, there you may be also' (John 14:1-3; see also 1 Thess. 4:13-18). In this sinful and dying world we could not ask for greater comfort than these promises.

But Christ's second coming is not just a comfort; it is also a spur to live a life of holiness. This is one of the evidences that we have been born again.

A hope so great and so divine
May trials well endure,
And purge the soul from sense and sin,
As Christ himself is pure.

(Scottish Paraphrases)

Or, to cite Isaac Watts:

> The men of grace have found
> Glory begun below;
> Celestial fruits on earthly ground
> From faith and hope may grow.

Every time you are tempted to sin — to explode in anger, to indulge in resentment, to live selfishly, to pander to a lust — think that Christ will come again and judge your actions, your motives, your innermost desires. That is the greatest possible incentive to holiness. Peter argues the same way in 2 Peter 3:10-13. The true Christian longs for the time when, at Christ's second coming, he will be made able never to sin again.

2. The Christian will be grateful to God

'Behold what manner of love the Father has bestowed on us, that we should be called children of God! [And we are].[3] **Therefore the world does not know us, because it did not know him'** (3:1). John is an aged man, close to death, but he has not lost the wonder of God's undeserved grace. 'Think of it,' he says, 'that such a righteous God should stoop down to the likes of us, whose very nature is a stench in his nostrils, and he lovingly calls us his children! By rights he should have nothing to do with us.' God has stooped down to save Noah, who was overcome by drunkenness; to Abraham who, out of fear, twice passed his wife off as his sister; to David, who was guilty of adultery, deception and murder by proxy; to Zacchaeus, who cheated people out of their livelihoods; to Paul who blasphemed the Saviour for so long and had his people put to death; to John Newton, caught up in the degradation of the slave-trade; and to all sinners down through the ages who have cried out in repentance for God's grace.

That is why the Scottish Paraphrases declare:

Behold the amazing gift of love
The Father hath bestowed
On us, the sinful sons of men,
To call us sons of God.

We are prone to be ungrateful, to lose the wonder of it all and to take God's grace for granted. Here is what one writer on the modern obsession with self-esteem says: 'Many Christians' self-esteem is terribly low... They even wonder how God could love such a person as themselves. They're amazed that God forgave their sins in the first place.'[4] So much for 'Amazing grace!' But the apostle John — like his namesake John Newton — was amazed that God could stoop down to the likes of him and redeem him from sin and death and hell. As the apostle John contemplated the love of God which has caused sinners to become his children, he may have added: 'And we are' (see the RSV, NRSV, NASB, NIV). If so, he was reminding himself and his readers of the wonders of the divine love in adopting children of Adam into God's own family.

If a beautiful and intelligent woman were to marry a grotesque and deformed man like the hunchback of Notre Dame, the world would be amazed. But God's adopting of sinners into his family is far more amazing. We must never lose the wonder of grace. To quote John Newton again, 'If I ever reach heaven I expect to find three wonders there: first, to meet some I had not thought to see there; second, to miss some I had thought to meet there; and third, the greatest wonder of all, to find myself there.'

3. The Christian is sustained by hope

'Beloved, now we are children of God; and it has not yet been revealed what we shall be, but we know that when

he is revealed, we shall be like him, for we shall see him as he is' (3:2). This is so wondrous a concept that Dr Martyn Lloyd-Jones once said that he felt sorry for anyone who has not had to spend a week with such a verse as this.[5] To cite the Scottish Paraphrase again:

> High is the rank we now possess,
> But higher we shall rise;
> Though what we shall hereafter be
> Is hid from mortal eyes.

Or, to quote Isaac Watts once more:

> There shall we see his face,
> And never, never sin;
> There from the rivers of his grace
> Drink endless pleasures in.

John is not so much telling us what heaven is like as telling us what the Christian will be like in heaven. The Christian is God's child now, but when Christ comes again, he will be like him for he shall see him face to face. Is that your hope? People of the world want to make it to the top, to make a name for themselves, to be well thought of, or to accumulate possessions, but Christians want to see Christ face to face and to be like him, never to sin again. That is the Christian hope.

The Christian will be made like Christ in his body: 'For our citizenship is in heaven, from which we also eagerly wait for the Saviour, the Lord Jesus Christ, who will transform our lowly body that it may be conformed to his glorious body, according to the working by which he is able even to subdue all things to himself' (Phil. 3:20-21). Your body may be in better shape than mine, but we all have the same problem — our bodies are subject to aches, pains, decay and finally death. It would be bad news were it not for Christ's own resurrection and the promise that all who belong to Christ will be raised as he was raised in a glorified body, never to die again.

Not only will the Christian be like Christ in his body, but also in righteousness. On this earth we are beset by sin, both within us and outside us. In heaven, however, the Christian will be unable to sin. The world regards that as a promise of eternal boredom: no poker machines, no wild parties, no crude jokes, none of the things that are supposed to make life enjoyable. The Christian is not so easily pleased. He knows that righteousness and happiness are inexorably linked together. The book of Revelation tells us: ' "Let us be *glad* and *rejoice* and give him glory, for the marriage of the Lamb has come, and his wife has made herself ready." And to her it was granted to be arrayed in fine linen, clean and bright, for the fine linen is the *righteous* acts of the saints' (Rev. 19:7-8). Later in the same book we read: 'Blessed are those who do his commandments, that they may have the right to the tree of life, and may enter through the gates into the city' (Rev. 22:14). Blessing — which is happiness obtained through God's approval — cannot be divorced from righteousness and obedience.

What does it mean to be a child of God, to be a member of God's family? It means that such a person believes in foundational truths, that God is righteous and that Christ is coming again. On the basis of faith in the righteous God who has revealed himself in his eternal Son Christ Jesus, we are to respond to what God has done with a righteous life, with gratitude for all God's grace and with hope that we shall see Christ and be made like him. Small wonder that John was astounded at the love of God!

8.
The child of God and sin

Please read 1 John 3:4-10

A quick rule-of-thumb way to tell whether a person is a Christian or not is to raise two questions:

1. What is your view of sin?
2. What is your view of Christ?

One can usually tell from the answers given to those two questions whether the person is a Christian or not. In 1 John 3:4-10 John looks at these two questions.

What about sin?

1. A definition

John declares simply that **'Sin is lawlessness'** (3:4). This is a basic definition. Sin is missing God's mark. God has a standard — his holy law as summarized, for example, in the Ten Commandments. We are to worship the one true God in his way; we are to reverence his name and keep his day; we are to honour our parents and to be loving, sexually pure, honest, truthful and contented in all things. Sin is falling short of that mark. The daughter says to the mother, 'I am moving in with my boyfriend.' The mother objects, but the daughter replies, 'It's all right, mother. Everybody is doing it.' How does God view such a situation? God says, 'I have a standard which is holy and right, and is designed for your benefit. If you violate that standard, you are sinning, no matter how many people agree with you.' As the *Shorter Catechism* puts it, 'Sin is any want of conformity unto, or transgression of, the law of God.'[1]

Sin is not to be defined as offending society's norms; it is not anti-social behaviour; it is not getting on the wrong side of the majority; it is not breaking the customs of etiquette. Of itself, it is not smoking on the bus or feeling bad about oneself. It matters little whether we have the support of most of our fellow citizens for we are warned, 'You shall not follow a crowd to do evil' (Exod. 23:2). Sin, in its very essence, is offending the revealed will of God.

2. Sin is of the devil

'He who sins is of the devil, for the devil has sinned from the beginning' (3:8). God created the world very good, but Satan rebelled and spoiled it all with sin. The devil is not some little red man in tights, with horns on his head and carrying a pitchfork. He is a fallen angel who was a murderer and liar from the beginning (John 8:44). Our pride, foul temper, selfish living, falsehood, impurity and waywardness are all our own responsibility (James 1:13-15), but every sin comes from Satan. A sinner may not even believe that Satan exists. That does not bother Satan. What matters is that the sinner belongs to Satan's kingdom.

What about Christ?

1. Christ's person

John says that **'In him there is no sin'** (3:5). A wretched
film, *The Last Temptation of Christ,* has tried to portray Jesus
as a sinner. But the truth is that Christ is, was and ever will be
sinless. For three years, John and the other apostles followed
Christ in very trying circumstances. Yet although they recog-
nized their own sins (e.g. 1:8,10; Luke 5:8), they detected no
sin in the Lord Jesus Christ (e.g. 3:5; 1 Peter 2:21-22). They
found nothing but goodness, truth and righteousness. Every
person on this earth has the same problem — he or she is a
sinner. 'No one is good but one, that is, God' (Luke 18:19).
God in the flesh — Christ Jesus — alone has escaped corrup-
tion from Adam. Christ alone is without sin, and so is able to
save rather than needing to be saved.

2. Christ's work

Christ was manifested **'to take away our sins'** (3:5). Jesus is,
in the words of John the Baptist, 'the Lamb of God who takes
away the sin of the world' (John 1:29). He takes away our sins
by the sacrifice of himself (Heb. 9:26). It is true that the sacri-
ficial death of Christ takes away the guilt of sinners who trust
in him, but it is also true that Christ not only came to take
away the guilt of sin but sin itself. This is made clear when
John later adds: **'For this purpose the Son of God was manifested, that he might destroy the works of the devil'** (3:8).
Satan desires to lead people away from God, to believe a lie.
This is reversed by Christ. Satan promotes sin, Christ righteousness; Satan delights in pride, Christ in humility. Satan says,

'Believe in yourself.' Christ says, 'Trust only in me.' Satan wants to bring wickedness, destruction, decay and death, but Christ came that we might have life and have it more abundantly (John 10:10). The devil has done untold damage and seeks to complete his work of woe, but Christ has restored his people and will complete his work of grace.

Living without sinning

Since we now know what sin is and where it comes from, and who Christ is and why he came to earth, there is obvious logic in John's blunt conclusion: **'Whoever abides in him does not sin. Whoever sins has neither seen him nor known him'** (3:6). Also, **'Whoever has been born of God does not sin, for his seed remains in him; and he cannot sin, because he has been born of God'** (3:9). But logical or not, this conclusion is startling. Is this not the same man who told us that 'If we say that we have no sin, we deceive ourselves, and the truth is not in us'? (1:8). Did John contradict himself? The Roman Catholic scholar Raymond E. Brown says, 'Yes,'[2] but we must emphatically declare, 'No, for the Scripture cannot be broken' (John 10:35). We are sinners (1:8), yet the Christian does not sin (3:6). Somehow, there is no contradiction.

Some have claimed that these verses from 1 John 3 teach a doctrine of Christian perfection. Throughout his life, John Wesley was convinced — rightly — of what he called 'the absolute impossibility of being half a Christian'.[3] Hence he taught, with a distinct lack of doctrinal clarity, that a Christian was obliged to be perfect and was in some sense capable of being so. However, it is sometimes difficult to be sure what Wesley meant — as, for example, when he declared, 'I do not contend for the term *sinless*, though I do not object against it.'[4]

In the next century, the nineteenth, the 'revivalist' Charles Finney went much further and taught that 'It is self-evident, that entire obedience to God's law is possible on the ground of natural ability.'[5] Yet Finney also backed off from pressing this too hard, and maintained that 'To overcome sin is the rule with everyone who is born of God, and that sin is only the exception; that the regenerate habitually live without sin, and fall into sin only at intervals, so few and far between, that in strong language it may be said in truth they do not sin.'[6]

The language of Christian perfectionism has — to put it mildly — been most unfortunate, and it has left a baneful legacy to the church. 'Victorious Life' teachings dominated conservative evangelicalism in the late nineteenth century and into the twentieth century. Charles Trumbull wrote a fawning biography of the father of Dispensationalism, Dr C. I. Scofield, and also pitted himself against the teaching of the *Shorter Catechism* that 'No mere man, since the fall, is able in this life, perfectly to keep the commandments of God; but doth daily break them in thought, word, and deed.'[7] Trumbull taught that 'It is the privilege of every Christian to live every day of his life without breaking the laws of God in known sin either in thought, word, or deed.'[8] Such teaching is contrary to Scripture, to experience and to common sense.

If Wesley, Finney and Trumbull have not proved altogether helpful in this matter, we are still left with the question: how are we to understand these verses in 1 John 3? The New International Version interprets as much as it translates, but it seems to get the idea right: 'No one who lives in him keeps on sinning [present continuous tense]. No one who continues to sin has either seen him or known him' (3:6). 'No one who is born of God will continue to sin [present continuous tense], because God's seed remains in him; he cannot go on sinning [present continuous tense], because he has been born of God' (3:9). If a person dwells habitually in sin, it is an indication that he or she has not been born again.

This is certainly taught elsewhere in Scripture. In Galatians 5:19-21 Paul lists the works of the flesh — all kinds of sexual immorality, idolatry, sorcery, hatred, contentions, and so on. Paul then declares emphatically that those who practise such things 'will not inherit the kingdom of God' (Gal. 5:21). It is not that one act of fornication, or one outburst of temper, or one bout of drunkenness will exclude us for ever from the kingdom. After all, David was guilty of adultery, even the normally meek Moses was guilty of bad temper and Noah fell into drunkenness after the flood. But it is certainly true that our lifestyle will be an indication of the state of our souls. We are not to be deceived, for 'Neither fornicators, nor idolaters, nor adulterers, nor homosexuals, nor sodomites, nor thieves, nor covetous [people], nor drunkards, nor revilers, nor extortioners will inherit the kingdom of God' (1 Cor. 6:9-10). This too is John's warning: **'Little children, let no one deceive you. He who practises righteousness is righteous, just as he is righteous'** (3:7). A believer may fall into sin, but he will not walk in it, and certainly will not wallow in it.

We cannot speak of what God has done for our souls unless he has also done something about our violent temper, our selfish attitudes, our indulgence in unlawful desires, our uncontrolled tongue and our simmering resentments. Justification by faith is not a licence to sin. Opposition to sin is the proof that God's seed (3:9) — by which John means either God's Word (1 Peter 1:23) or, more probably, God's Spirit (John 3:3,5,6) — indwells us and that we are born again. To say complacently, 'Oh, yes, I am a Christian,' while we cannot keep a civil tongue in our heads, or while we continue to delight in gossip, or while we are refusing to pay any attention to a clear command in Scripture, is to deceive ourselves. In Paul's terms, we are slaves to sin or slaves to righteousness; there is no middle ground (Rom. 6).

In 1886 the Anglican commentator Alfred Plummer put it well: 'Although the believer sometimes sins, yet not sin, but opposition to sin, is the ruling principle of his life; for whenever he sins he confesses it, and wins forgiveness, and perseveres with his self-purification. But the habitual sinner does none of these things: sin is his ruling principle. And this could not be the case if he had ever really known Christ.'[9] There are only two kinds of people in God's sight, and they are distinguished by their attitude — in word and deed — to sin and to Christ.

It is a clear and decisive test that John has given to us: **'In this the children of God and the children of the devil are manifest: whoever does not practise righteousness is not of God, nor is he who does not love his brother'** (3:10). Here is one of the ways in which we can tell the child of God from the child of the devil. We are usually very ready to believe that other people are sinners, but we must test ourselves first. If you habitually follow after sin and delight in it, you have no reason to believe you belong to God in a saving sense. Practising righteousness is not just a good or happy thing, something to be recommended, nor even the ideal for the Christian — it is a necessary proof that we have indeed been born again. 1 John is a book about tests, and Robert Murray M'Cheyne had good reason to lament that 'More souls are lost through want of consideration than in any other way.'[10] Let that not be said of us. Let us test ourselves!

9.
Love one another

Please read 1 John 3:11-18

John is always keen to show that the various tests of the Christian life go together. Hence he combines the two tests of righteousness and love: **'Whoever does not practise righteousness is not of God, nor is he who does not love his brother'** (3:10). He then develops the test of love. One of the problems with love is that everybody agrees with it. 'What the world needs now is love, sweet love,' goes the song, and not too many will register their disapproval. The problem, of course, lies in defining what love is. From 1 Corinthians 13, love might be defined as a holy giving of oneself. To the world, love is sometimes equated with sex, sometimes with agreeing with everyone (e.g. if a Christian does not agree with Hindus or homosexuals he is said to be without love), or sometimes with a general feeling of vague benevolence. We desperately need to keep in mind what the Bible means by 'love'.

The command to love

John declares, **'For this is the message that you heard from the beginning, that we should love one another'** (3:11). Calvin put it very clearly: 'We cannot hurt, slander, mock, despise, or in any way offend one of our brethren without at the same time hurting, slandering, mocking, despising Christ in him. We cannot be at variance with our brethren without at the same time being at variance with Christ. We cannot love Christ without loving him in our brethren.'[1]

Love is not the cause of salvation, but it is the fruit of it. Indeed, it is the necessary fruit of God's having worked in our lives in a saving way: **'We know that we have passed from death to life, because we love the brethren. He who does not love his brother abides in death'** (3:14). This verse does not contain the whole story, but one of the evidences that a person is a Christian is that he loves other Christians.

Our natural spiritual state is one of death (John 5:24-25; Eph. 2:1-3). The person who is born again of the Spirit of God has passed from spiritual death to spiritual life. One of the most convincing evidences that this has taken place in a person is that he or she experiences a new and holy concern for the welfare of those who profess the same faith in Christ Jesus. A person who does not love Christians is himself not a Christian. John is not mincing his words. He is echoing the teaching of the Sermon on the Mount (see Matt. 5:21-26) that hatred in the heart is, in fact, murderous in the sight of God, and is an indication that a person is as yet in an unregenerate condition. Love is from God.

Cain's murderous example

John says we are to love one another, **'not as Cain who was of the wicked one and murdered his brother. And why did he murder him? Because his works were evil and his brother's righteous. Do not marvel, my brethren, if the world hates you'** (3:12-13). Back in Genesis 3 we read that Adam and Eve fell into the basic sin of disobeying God's Word. This had far-reaching and drastic consequences. In Genesis 4 Cain

butchered his own brother, Abel, and ever since then the world
has hated Christians. Just press your unbelieving friends and
neighbours on any point of the Christian faith, and you will
see how quickly the mildest temperament can become very
antagonistic. Cain was hostile to Abel for no other reason than
that Abel was right with God and Cain was not. That was all
the reason which Cain needed.

We cannot be complacent here and say, 'Well, I have never
cut anyone's throat.' There is more to it than that. The envy
that leads to murder is there in all of us, and has to be put to
death. What about snubbing someone in order to avenge ourselves of some slight, real or imaginary? Or slandering someone when we are not even sure of the facts? Or resenting someone because we have been hurt or let down? 'Oh, those things
are not murder,' you might reply. True, but God says that they
indicate a murderous heart: **'Whoever hates his brother is a
murderer'** (3:15). Cain and Abel once played together as
brothers, but Cain failed to control his envy of Abel, and finally murdered him. Most murders involve someone who at
one stage loved someone else in some way, but came to murder him or her. Such is the wickedness of the human heart.
Such sin reflects the character of Satan himself (John 8:44).

Even indifference to other people's lives is condemned in
Scripture:

Deliver those who are drawn toward death,
And hold back those stumbling to the slaughter.
If you say, 'Surely we did not know this,'
Does not he who weighs the hearts consider it?
He who keeps your soul, does he not know it?
And will he not render to each man according to his
    deeds?

(Prov. 24:11-12).

Esther delivered her people from death, Obadiah hid the prophets of the Lord (1 Kings 18:4), Ebed-Melech spoke out for
Jeremiah and helped him when it was inviting trouble to do so
(Jer. 38:1-13) and Paul's nephew intervened to save the great
apostle (Acts 23:16-22). A Christian cannot remain silent when
terrible things are happening — whether it be the consigning
of Jews to gas ovens in Nazi Germany or the wanton destruction of unborn life today. Modern secular man is becoming
increasingly callous. Australians professed to be shocked not
long ago when a twelve-year-old boy was hit by a motor ve-
hicle and left to die by the side of the road in Sydney — in full
view of the traffic — because people were too indifferent to
offer practical love. But this is a story which is sadly becoming
all too common in the modern world.

The supreme example of love

The Christian ought to know love far better than the world:
**'By this we know love, because he laid down his life for us.
And we also ought to lay down our lives for the brethren'**
(3:16). We can only love through Christ; humanistic love is
not enough. The supreme act of love is Christ's giving of himself for his sinful people (see Gal. 2:20; Eph. 5:2,25). We cannot pay the penalty for anyone's sin in that same sense, but
John still says that we ought to lay down our lives for the
brethren. To that extent, we are to imitate the sacrifice of Christ.
Taken literally, this is obviously not an everyday event — in
fact, we could only do it once! But it shows us how serious
John is about love. When the playboy tells the girl, 'I love
you', what he actually means is 'I love me and I want you.'
True love, as a contrast, takes self-giving to the point, if necessary, of dying for the one who is beloved. There was a case
in France in World War II where a Jewish woman had been

condemned to death by the Nazis, but a Russian Orthodox nun, Mother Maria, took her place. Over the centuries, thousands of missionaries have perished — either through martyrdom or sickness — in order to bring the gospel to other people. This is obeying Christ: 'Greater love has no one than this, than to lay down one's life for his friends' (John 15:13). This love is more important than the actual act of self-sacrifice itself (1 Cor. 13:3).

The practicalities of day-to-day love

John quickly takes us from the heroic and supreme example of self-sacrifice to the more mundane level of living each day: **'But whoever has this world's goods, and sees his brother in need, and shuts up his heart from him, how does the love of God abide in him? My little children, let us not love in word or in tongue, but in deed and in truth'** (3:17-18). We are rarely called upon to die for someone; we are constantly called upon to live for someone. We are to feed the hungry, give blankets to the needy, give what we can to whom we can, wipe the dishes, bathe the children and be considerate when others in the family are feeling frayed around the edges.

The Bible is a very down-to-earth book. James is as practical as John: 'If a brother or sister is naked and destitute of daily food, and one of you says to them, "Depart in peace, be warmed and filled," but you do not give them the things which are needed for the body, what does it profit? Thus also faith by itself, if it does not have works, is dead' (James 2:15-17). That is simply telling us to do something for the other person. We would be horrified if, over a week, we counted up what we do for ourselves and compared it to what we do for others.

The early church was renowned not only for its doctrinal purity but also its practical charity. The emperor Julian the

Apostate complained during his short reign from A.D. 361 to 363 that 'The impious Galileans support not only their own poor but ours as well.' That is the kind of love that John had in mind — the love of the Christians was having an impact on their society, to Julian's chagrin. The trouble is that people generally are fond of the idea of loving humanity, but we are not so good at making that concrete in day-to-day life:

> To love the world to me's no chore;
> My big trouble is the man next door!

Bertrand Russell used to pontificate to the nations about how they should live together in peace and harmony, but treated his succession of wives very shabbily. We who profess the precious name of Christ must test ourselves: do we love those who belong to him? Well might we take to heart 'Rabbi' Duncan's stricture that 'If you are without love, then the church bell is as good a Christian as you.'[2]

10.
Dealing with doubt

Please read 1 John 3:19-24

We can easily sing, 'Blessed assurance! Jesus is mine,' but a lingering doubt may still remain: 'Is Jesus really mine?' Pastorally, it is difficult to deal with people who think that they are Christians when they are not, or with those who doubt whether they are Christians but who seem to be. It is always much easier to deal with people who are Christians and know they are, or with those who are not Christians and know that they are not. Throughout his letter, John has been dealing with Christians who stand in need of assurance.

The three tests reviewed

John raises three tests in this section of his epistle.

1. Obedience

John asserts that **'We keep his commandments and do those things that are pleasing in his sight'** (3:22). This kind of obedience is, as Robert Candlish puts it, 'not as seeking acceptance, but as already accepted; not as a servant on trial, but as a son abiding in the house evermore.'[1] As a result, this kind of obedience ministers to our assurance in Christ. But if obeying God's Word does not interest you, you are not a Christian.

2. Right doctrine

John tells us that **'This is his commandment: that we should believe on the name of his Son Jesus Christ'** (3:23). A Christian is not just any person who happens to be pleasant or easy to get along with. A man claimed in our local newspaper recently that he was 'a non-practising Christian', and then proceeded to berate all those who dared to eat meat (contrary to 1 Timothy 4:1-5)! A Christian is first and foremost one who believes that the man Jesus of Nazareth is the Christ, the Anointed One, the Messiah, the one promised in the Old Testament (Dan. 9:25-26). He is God's eternal Son who has become man.

3. Love

John reminds us again that we are to **'love one another, as he** [Christ] **gave us commandment'** (3:23).

The *Westminster Confession of Faith* has some wise words on the subject of Christian assurance: 'This certainty is not a bare conjectural and probable persuasion grounded upon a fallible hope; but an infallible assurance of faith founded upon the divine truth of the promises of salvation, the inward evidence of those graces unto which these promises are made, the testimony of the Spirit of adoption witnessing with our spirits that we are the children of God, which Spirit is the earnest of our inheritance, whereby we are sealed to the day of redemption.'[2]

The Confession tells us that there is one objective ground of assurance — God's promises in the gospel (e.g. John 3:16); and two subjective grounds — the inward evidences or fruits of grace (e.g. the tests of 1 John) and the inward testimony of the Holy Spirit testifying to our spirits that we are children of God (e.g. Rom. 8:16). These three grounds for assurance cannot be separated, and must be understood in the order in which they appear in the Confession. We must look first to the gospel promises in Christ before we try to discern the fruit of the Spirit in our lives or the Spirit's testimony to our spirits. As Thomas Brooks put it, 'Let thy eye and heart, first, most, and last, be fixed upon Christ, then will assurance bed and board with thee.'[3]

It is also worth our while to quote Richard Baxter, who advised his parishioners to 'Be sure that the first and far greater part of your time, pains, and care, and enquiries, be for the getting and increasing of your grace, than for the discerning it... See that you ask ten times at least, "How should I get or increase my faith, my love to Christ, and to his people?" for once that you ask, "How shall I know that I believe or love?" '[4]

What the Puritans were saying is that the tests of 1 John are not the first grounds of assurance for the Christian. The first ground is the gospel itself. But the three tests together are a necessary indication to us that the gospel is truly ours. Then we must also add, as the apostle John does, that keeping the commandments and experiencing the Spirit reveal that we belong to God: **'Now he who keeps his commandments abides in him, and he in him. And by this we know that he abides in us, by the Spirit whom he has given us'** (3:24). It is important that we understand that the three tests are indivisible — all three are binding on us; we cannot have one without the whole three. It is also vital that we see how the three tests fit in with the other grounds of assurance.

A clear conscience and a sense of assurance

If we possess a clear conscience, we will know assurance. It is sin that mars our sense of assurance, just as it mars everything else. **'Beloved, if our heart does not condemn us, we have confidence toward God. And whatever we ask we receive from him'** (3:21-22). The Bible sets much store by a clear conscience. In the book of Hebrews we read, 'For if the blood of bulls and goats and the ashes of a heifer, sprinkling the unclean, sanctifies for the purifying of the flesh, how much more shall the blood of Christ, who through the eternal Spirit offered himself without spot to God, cleanse your conscience from dead works to serve the living God?' (Heb. 9:13-14). It is the blood of Christ that gives the Christian a clear conscience — hence the admonition: 'Let us draw near with a true heart in full assurance of faith, having our hearts sprinkled from an evil conscience and our bodies washed with pure water' (Heb. 10:22).

Christ's death not only pays the penalty for sin, but also cleanses the sinner's conscience. The sinner thus comes to Christ as John Newton did:

With my burden I begin:
Lord, remove this load of sin;
Let thy blood, for sinners spilt,
Set my conscience free from guilt.

In the courts of heaven, the sinner's record is wiped clean, and in the sinner's guilty conscience there is a sense of cleansing for the first time. This is true peace.

This is to be the norm for the Christian. He has a new freedom and confidence in prayer; the old barriers are down. The Christian takes Christ at his word: 'These things I have spoken

to you, that in me you may have peace. In the world you will
have tribulation; but be of good cheer, I have overcome the
world' (John 16:33). If that kind of assurance and confidence
is not there, something is wrong. Robert Candlish is quite correct in saying, 'I cannot look my God in the face if I cannot
look myself in the face.'⁵ Normally, a clear conscience before
God is a good sign, provided the three tests of right belief,
love and obedience are passed in some real measure.

The Christian conscience is not infallible, and John Owen
made the perceptive comment that 'To *be holy* is necessary;
to *know it*, sometimes a temptation.'⁶ Yet it is accepted in Scripture that conscience is something that is worthy and that can
be a reliable indicator of spiritual reality. The apostle Peter
writes, 'But sanctify the Lord God in your hearts, and always
be ready to give a defence to everyone who asks you a reason
for the hope that is in you, with meekness and fear; having a
good conscience, that when they defame you as evildoers, those
who revile your good conduct in Christ may be ashamed' (1 Peter 3:15-16). Paul also took the claims of conscience very se-
riously (Acts 18:6; 20:26; 23:1; 24:16; 2 Tim. 1:3). In fact,
those who refuse to believe the claims of Christ are still not
devoid of conscience. The scribes and Pharisees once brought
an adulterous woman to Jesus in order to test and accuse him,
but when Jesus declared, 'He who is without sin among you,
let him throw a stone at her first', they were convicted by their
consciences and slunk away (John 8:7-9). Our consciences
can either accuse or excuse us (see Rom. 2:14-16).

The over-sensitive conscience

An over-sensitive conscience can be an awkward pastoral problem: **'And by this we know that we are of the truth, and
shall assure our hearts before him. For if our heart**

condemns us, God is greater than our heart, and knows all things' (3:19-20). There has been some dispute about these words. Augustine and Calvin claimed that John was saying that God's judgement is more severe than ours, and Robert Candlish agrees with this interpretation, commenting that 'I must be able to acquit myself of guilt if I would reckon on his acquitting me of guilt.'[7] Dr Martyn Lloyd-Jones also thinks that this verse is not meant to comfort but to warn us. He says, 'I have known a drunken man tell me that he is relying upon the Cross.'[8] It is true that if we are tolerating what is questionable, our hearts condemn us, and God's judgement is far more searching that ours could ever be. 1 John was written both to test its readers and to reassure those who are true Christians. But the context here seems to favour Luther's view that John is reassuring his readers rather than challenging them.

Sometimes one hears that the final authority for Roman Catholics is the pope, but for Protestants it is conscience. John Henry Newman once gained some notoriety amongst his fellow Roman Catholics by declaring that if he were obliged to bring religion into after-dinner toasts, he would drink 'to the Pope, if you please — still, to Conscience first, and to the Pope afterwards'.[9] Be that as it may, the final authority for Protestants is neither conscience nor the pope but Scripture, God's inerrant Word. If your conscience tells you that you are all right while you are out of step with Scripture, then your conscience is sinfully astray. In 1 Corinthians 4:3-4, for example, the apostle Paul holds out the possibility that his conscience may not be rigorous enough. An adulterous woman who says to herself, 'I have done no wickedness' is greatly deluded (Prov. 30:20), as was the rich young ruler who thought he had kept the commandments from his youth (Luke 18:18-21).

John, however, appears to be referring to the opposite problem, to the possibility that one's conscience is too tender, to the point that true Christians may feel self-condemned. They may read 1 John 3:6 and think of their sins and wonder, 'How could I have done those things, said those things, thought those things, and still be a Christian?' Or perhaps they read verses about loving the brethren and even laying down our lives for them (3:14,16), and they say to themselves, 'I could not even speak to my wife in a civil way this morning. How can I kid myself that my love is so great that I could die for others?' They may believe; they may be able to say with Martha, 'Yes, Lord, I believe that you are the Christ, the Son of God, who is to come into the world' (John 11:27). But they feel, often with ample justification, that their lives are disorderly, unloving and lacking in much commendation to the unbelieving world. Thomas Brooks called assurance 'the suburbs of paradise', but these Christians feel that they are living out in the bush. Does the Scripture have anything to say to such people? Yes, it does.

1. A Christian wants to know whether his faith is true or not

Hence he prays with David,

> Search me, O God, and know my heart;
> Try me, and know my anxieties;
> And see if there is any wicked way in me,
> And lead me in the way everlasting
>
> (Ps. 139:23-24).

The last thing that an unbeliever wants is for his conscience to be thoroughly searched in the way that David prayed. An unbeliever does not want to know about his sins; he only wants a reassurance that he is all right and has nothing to worry about. Psalm 139 is the prayer of a man with an awakened conscience, of a good man who wants to know the worst about himself.

'Rabbi' Duncan had a wise saying: 'There's nobody perfect. That's the believer's bed of thorns. That's the hypocrite's couch of ease.'[10]

2. Recall the character of God

That seems to be the point of verse 20. Something similar is found in Paul's treatment of assurance in Romans 8: 'What then shall we say to these things? If God is for us, who can be against us? He who did not spare his own Son, but delivered him up for us all, how shall he not with him also freely give us all things?' (Rom. 8:31-32). Sometimes we need to be reminded of God's awful holiness; sometimes we need to be reminded of his abounding graciousness. 'The Lord knows those who are his' (2 Tim. 2:19), even if, for a time, they feel self-condemned.

3. Do not brood and stagnate

Richard Baxter used to advise: 'He that wants assurance must not stand still, but exercise his graces till his doubts vanish.' John Owen had similar words of advice: 'Take heed of spending time in complaints when vigorous actings of grace are your duty.'[11] Assurance will not be nurtured through self-pity or depression. Moping is no substitute for working.

Finally, assurance should come with a clear, as opposed to a complacent, conscience before God. It is not necessarily instantaneous, and may need to be sought again and again. John Owen himself only came to assurance after a melancholy period of some five years. An unknown preacher — standing in for Edmund Calamy at Aldermandbury Chapel — expounded Matthew 8:26 in a way that spoke to him, and from that time on, he enjoyed a new assurance that he was a child of God.[12]

11.
Testing the spirits

Please read 1 John 4:1-6

John makes it clear that a true Christian must possess a measure of discernment, a God-given capacity to tell truth from error. A Christian may not have waded through Charles Hodge's three-volume *Systematic Theology*, but he does need to have grasped the basics of God's revelation. Not all teaching, even inside the church, is from God. One is tempted to say these days that much teaching about Christ, even inside the church, is not from God. John has written of the true Christ in 1 John 1:1-4 and 2:18-27, and now returns to this doctrinal test to develop it a little further.

The fact of false teaching

Christians are warned, with affection as those who are **'be-loved'**, that **'Many false prophets have gone out into the world'** (4:1). There are no true prophets today because prophets, together with apostles, constitute the foundation of the church (Eph. 2:20). As such, they received direct revelation from God.[1] This has come to us in written form, and the canon of Scripture is now closed. We are not to add to, nor detract from, the Scripture as the fully authoritative and sufficient Word of God. Therefore, anyone who claims to be a prophet today in this sense can be safely rejected. However, we still need to heed the biblical warnings about false teachers.

All through Scripture we find similar warnings. False teachers may even perform signs and wonders (Deut. 13:1-2; Matt. 24:24; 2 Thess. 2:9), but they are not to be heeded. What matters is truth: ' "But the prophet who presumes to speak a word in my name, which I have not commanded him to speak, or who speaks in the name of other gods, that prophet shall die." And if you say in your heart, "How shall we know the word which the LORD has not spoken?" — when a prophet speaks in the name of the LORD, if the thing does not happen or come to pass, that is the thing which the LORD has not spoken: the prophet has spoken it presumptuously; you shall not be afraid of him' (Deut. 18:20-22).

False teachers tend to tell unregenerate people exactly what they want to hear. They flatter those who pay no attention to God's claims on their lives.

> Thus says the LORD of hosts:
> 'Do not listen to the words of the prophets who proph-
> esy to you.
> They make you worthless;
> They speak a vision of their own heart,
> Not from the mouth of the LORD.
> They continually say to those who despise me,
> "The LORD has said, 'You shall have peace' ";
> And to everyone who walks according to the dictates of
> his own heart, they say,
> "No evil shall come upon you" '
>
> (Jer. 23:16-17).

Surely the reader has been to the funeral of a rank unbeliever, and has been assured by the preacher that the deceased was now in heaven. Robert Schuller tells people that they are beautiful, Oral Roberts says that something good is going to happen to them, while Kenneth Copeland promises them health, wealth and prosperity. As a contrast, Scripture warns us about prophets who claim that there is peace when, in fact, there is no peace (Jer. 6:14; 8:11; 28:9; Ezek.13:10,16; Micah 3:5).

False teachers have arisen from within the leadership of the church (Acts 20:29-30). Some will arise and give heed to deceiving spirits and doctrines of demons, and forbid Christians to marry and command them to abstain from certain foods (1 Tim. 4:1-5). They will preach a different Jesus, a different spirit and a different gospel, but they will appear as angels of light (2 Cor. 11:3-4,13-15). They will not come with the label 'False Prophet' on their foreheads, or with publicity in neon lights: 'Come and hear a false prophet tonight.' Instead, they will *secretly* bring in destructive heresies and lead people astray (2 Peter 2:1). It is a particularly unpleasant fact of church life that not all teaching that presents itself as Christian is in fact Christian. We need to be aware of this, especially in these ecumenical days when people are so fond of playing down any differences of belief. There are false teachers in the professing church of the Lord Jesus Christ, in all denominations.

If there is such a thing as truth, there is also such a thing as falsehood. When Jeremiah proclaimed that the exile in Babylon would last seventy years (Jer. 25:11) and Hananiah declared that it would last two years (Jer. 28:1-4), these men were not sharing their complementary insights. One was proclaiming the truth of God and the other was lying in the name of God.

Responding with discernment and confidence

To respond properly to false teaching, the Christian requires both discernment and confidence.

Discernment

With regard to discernment, the Christian is not to believe every spirit but to **'test the spirits'** (4:1). There is nothing Christian about being gullible. Discernment is a Christian grace. We are to test all things and hold fast to what is good (1 Thess. 5:21). The risen and ascended Lord Jesus had some critical things to say about the church at Ephesus, but he did commend it because it had 'tested those who say they are apostles and are not, and have found them liars' (Rev. 2:2). Jesus warned us that the wolves would come in sheep's clothing (Matt. 7:15). And we need to remember that John says that 'many' false prophets had gone out into the world. False prophets and false teachers will not necessarily consist of a small and despised minority — they may well carry with them the intimidation which goes with having attracted considerable numerical support.

At times the exercise of discernment should be relatively easy. Jay Adams tells how he was once driving through Texas and heard a preacher on the car radio invite listeners to 'Stay tuned to this programme because at the end of the message I will tell you how to obtain an autographed picture of Jesus Christ.' This offer was repeated, and — we ought not to be surprised — the listener was encouraged to include a gift to support the 'ministry' of the preacher.[2] Anyone with a modicum of common sense, let alone the indwelling Holy Spirit, ought to have been able to tell that the preacher on the radio was a confidence trickster. As John Wesley lamented, in a way that G. K. Chesterton might have appreciated, 'If a man will not believe God, he will believe anything. Why he may believe a man could put himself into a quart bottle.'[3]

At other times, the task of being discerning may require a little more intellectual and spiritual dexterity. For example, consider what William Barclay has to say on three issues, and pick out what is wrong:

1. On the *atonement*: 'I began to see the tremendous thing, the fact that Jesus came, not to change God's attitude to men, but, to demonstrate God's attitude to men, to show men at the cost of the Cross what God is like.'[4]

2. On the *resurrection*: 'I am certain that something happened to make Jesus available for all time in all places to those who love him and believe.'[5]

3. On *judgement*: 'Nothing less than a world is enough for the love of God.'[6]

We do not need a carping, hyper-critical spirit, which can find nothing but error and sin in others. Yet we do need a godly discernment. Error will always come dressed up as truth, even with clerical collars and mitres. We are under obligation to *love* all humanity; we are under no obligation to *believe* all humanity. For a mechanic to know what is wrong with your car, he needs to know something about engines; for a doctor to heal your illness, he needs to know something about how the human body works; and for a Christian to discern truth from error, he needs to know his Bible. We may not immediately grasp all the intricacies of Daniel 11, but we must be able to test the spirits by the Word of God.

Confidence

The second feature of the Christian's response to false teaching concerns confidence. John writes, **'You are of God, little children, and have overcome them, because he who is in you is greater than he who is in the world'** (4:4). It is easy to be overawed by someone who sounds 'super-spiritual', who seems to have something that you do not have. The Gnostics of John's day, and later, put so-called knowledge above faith. They taught a system of passwords, the knowledge of which would enable the purified soul to journey through the aeons which were supposedly between God and the cosmos.

According to Irenaeus, the second-century Gnostic Valentinus claimed that God (who, he said, is pure spirit and cannot be known) was lonely, so he made two divine beings called 'spirit aeons'. Eventually, there came to be thirty aeons. The number 'thirty' could be arrived at by various means:

1. Adding together the numbers from the parable of the workers in the vineyard in Matthew 20:1-16 (the 1st, 3rd, 6th, 9th, and 11th hours); or

2. Adding together the number of Christ's apostles, or his age while teaching in the temple (i.e. twelve), to the length of time that he remained with his disciples after the resurrection (which Valentinus calculated at eighteen months!) or to the combined numerical value of the first two letters in Jesus' name in Greek (i.e. eighteen).

Fortunately, Irenaeus was not easily intimidated by this parade of 'knowledge' and dismissed it all as 'baseless speculations' and 'perverse interpretations and deceitful expositions'![7] But Christians may feel a little weak in the presence of someone who glibly declares, 'I was talking to the Lord this morning and he told me such and such.' Such a person seems closer to the Lord than we are, yet it may have no more substance to it than the Gnostic speculations of old. The same can be said for those who seek to overawe you with their sure-fire grasp of biblical prophecies and give you a timetable for what is about to take place.

John says, 'If you are a Christian, you have the Holy Spirit. The Holy Spirit is greater than the spirits of this world which are behind all heresies. Be strong; be confident. You are on the winning side.' This is a concept to seize hold of in the trials of life. On 7 March 1553 Calvin quoted 'He who dwells in you is stronger than the world' in a letter to five prisoners at Lyons who were facing death through burning at the stake for heresy.[8] Calvin's letters to his persecuted brethren, which were devoid of false hope and platitudes and based squarely on the Word of God, proved to be a great comfort to them.

A clear faith banishes fear. When the King of Syria sought to capture the prophet Elisha in the city of Dothan, Elisha's servant saw the army with the horses and chariots around the city, and hit the panic button: 'Alas, my master! What shall we do?' Elisha responded, 'Do not fear, for those who are with us are more than those who are with them.' Then Elisha prayed, 'LORD, I pray, open his eyes that he may see.' The result was that the Lord opened the eyes of the young man, and he saw that the mountain was full of horses and chariots of fire around Elisha (2 Kings 6:15-17). There is a spiritual battle going on, and the Christian needs to be confident that he is on the winning side. Christ will reign at his Father's right hand until he makes all his enemies his footstool (Ps. 110:1). Such confidence will keep us from wavering.

Two tests

It is all very well to say that we must have discernment and confidence, but how can we be confident that we are discerning? John gives us two tests: **'By this you know the Spirit of God: every spirit that confesses that Jesus Christ has come in the flesh is of God, and every spirit that does not confess that Jesus Christ has come in the flesh is not of God. And this is the spirit of the Antichrist, which you have heard was coming, and is now already in the world'** (4:2-3).

Anyone who does not confess the man Jesus as the Christ (the Messiah) come in the flesh is of the Antichrist who rules the world (see 1 Cor. 12:1-3). They are proclaiming *a* Christ instead of *the true* Christ. John tells us very clearly the source from which false religious teachers derive their authority: **'They are of the world. Therefore they speak as of the world, and the world hears them'** (4:5).

1. A right view of Christ

This test eliminates a whole host of heretics:

The Gnostics, who believed that the divine Christ descended on the man Jesus, then left him before the crucifixion;

The New Age movement, which believes that the Christ spirit has descended upon many great men down through the ages, with Jesus of Nazareth just being one among many;

Liberal theologians who refuse to say that Jesus Christ is the God-man, the one and only mediator between God and man;

Cults such as the Jehovah's Witnesses, the Christadelphians and the Mormons which deny that in Christ all the fulness of the Deity dwells bodily (Col. 2:9).

The test is not whether a person or a group uses Christian terms, but which Christ is confessed. Many — probably most — seminaries in the Western world belong to the Antichrist. The Antichrist is not necessarily an insidious bureaucrat working for the United Nations. The Greek word *'anti'* means 'instead of'. In Matthew 20:28, for example, Jesus declares that 'The Son of Man did not come to be served, but to serve, and

to give his life a ransom for *[anti]* many.' What he means is
that he came to give his life instead of many — he would die
that many would live. To believe in the wrong Christ — one
who is less than the God-man of history and Scripture — is to
belong to Antichrist. To believe in the wrong Christ is to perish.

So much rests on the reality of the incarnation. If Christ did
not come in the flesh because the flesh is evil, then logically it
is not only the incarnation which is dismissed. The reality of
Christ's sufferings and death is also called into question, as is
the reality of Christ's physical resurrection from the dead. A
right understanding of the work of the Lord Jesus depends on
a right understanding of his person.

2. Adherence to the apostolic Word

**'We are of God. He who knows God hears us; he who is
not of God does not hear us. By this we know the spirit of
truth and the spirit of error'** (4:6). The NIV and the GNB
are probably correct in capitalizing 'the Spirit of truth' to refer to the Holy Spirit. John is saying that 'We apostles are of
God' and the one who hears 'us', i.e. the apostles, has the
Spirit of truth who was promised by Jesus (John 14:17; 15:26;
16:13). The one who thinks that he knows the mind of God
better than the apostles shows that he is not right with God. A
Christian is one who tests all teachings by the standard of the
Word of God (see Acts 17:11). When Christians at Thessalonica
received the word of the apostle Paul, they welcomed it not as
the word of men but as the word of God (1 Thess. 2:13).

All over the church — let alone the world — there are
people who think that they know better than the Word of God.
We find this on all sorts of issues — such as the way of salvation, the existence of hell, the practice of homosexuality, or
the wisdom of corporal discipline. We are to test all teachers
not by their charm, their liveliness, their intelligence, their

plausibility, the attractiveness of their presentation, or their capacity to hold an audience by their powers of oratory. What matters is the *content* of their teaching. The point is that the one who is of God hears God's words, while the one who is not of God rejects God's words (John 8:47; 10:4-5,26-27).

When the twelve-volume work *The Fundamentals* was released in 1910-1915, the fundamentals of the Christian faith were deemed to be the authority of the Bible, the deity of Christ, his virgin birth, his miracles and his resurrection, and his second coming. You can believe all those things and still not be a Christian,[9] but a Christian does believe all those things. Those who oppose those fundamentals are not postulating a slightly different, perhaps more modern, version of Christianity. They are simply not Christian at all.

We need to test all teachers, not by whether they come with imprimaturs from the Vatican or from the World Council of Churches, but by these God-given tests. Do they proclaim the God-man Jesus Christ? And do they seek to hold to the Word of God in doctrine and practice? You and I need discernment and we need confidence in the Spirit.

12.
Love is of God

Please read 1 John 4:7-21

John's method in this epistle is to raise each issue — whether the person of Christ, love for his people, or obedience to his commandments — deal with it, then return to the theme later and develop it further. John has already dealt with the subject of love in 1 John 2:7-11 and then again in 3:11-18. Now, in chapter 4:7-21 it is tackled yet again, this time in greater detail. Biblical love is never divorced from biblical faith. Even in this section on love, John is quick to point out the apostolic testimony to the sending of the divine Saviour into the world (4:14) and the need to confess that Jesus is the Son of God (4:15). Yet it is small wonder that Augustine said of John in this first epistle: 'He has spoken many words, and nearly all are about love.'[1] It is in his sermon series on 1 John that Augustine delivered his famous and perhaps not altogether helpful precept: 'Love, and do what you will.'[2]

God is love

God's very nature is love: **'Beloved, let us love one another, for love is of God; and everyone who loves is born of God and knows God. He who does not love does not know God, for God is love'** (4:7-8). This is repeated in verse 16: **'And**

**we have known and believed the love that God has for us.
God is love, and he who abides in love abides in God, and
God in him.'** Verse 19 adds, **'We love [him] because he
first loved us.'**[3] God is the source and the origin of love. By
ourselves, we are unable to come to love God because we are
alienated from him (Col. 1:21). Out of love for his people,
God chose them, not for anything in them, but solely because
of his love (Deut. 7:7-8). There is no love apart from God. We
only know God because he knows us first (Gal. 4:9); we only
love him because he placed his love in us first (4:10,19). God's
very nature is love. It is not just that God loves — he does
(John 3:16; Rom. 5:8) — but that he is love.

Love is not mawkish or sentimental; it is not a feeling which
exists without moral standards. Even Robert Candlish seems
to have been in error here. He maintains that love is not created as light is.[4] According to Candlish, God declared, 'Let
there be light,' but there is no declaration, 'Let there be love.'
But this is a false dichotomy. When the Bible states that 'God
is light' (1:5), it is not echoing Genesis 1. 'Light' in Genesis 1
is day as opposed to night; 'light' in 1 John 1:5 is holiness as
opposed to evil. God does not create his own holiness. Rather,
the God who is light is also love. There is no contradiction
between the God who is a consuming fire (Heb. 12:29) and
the God who loves so much that he gives to the uttermost. It
is not that love is God's basic attribute; all of his attributes go
together.

Because God is love, there is no love apart from God. The
non-Christian can love in a certain sense, as a result of God's
common grace. As Jesus said, 'But if you love those who love
you, what credit is that to you? For even sinners love those
who love them. And if you do good to those who do good to
you, what credit is that to you? For even sinners do the same.
And if you lend to those from whom you hope to receive back,
what credit is that to you? For even sinners lend to sinners to

receive as much back' (Luke 6:32-33). They buy each other a beer in the hope of getting one back and earning a reputation for being a good fellow. They help their friends get a taxi home when they have drunk too much to drive themselves. We all find it easy to love those who respond to us and who think that we are wonderful. In fact, at times unbelievers — such as those on the island of Malta in Paul's day — can perform acts of 'unusual kindness' (Acts 28:2). All of this makes life on earth more tolerable than it would otherwise be, but it is not Christian love.

God's love manifested

Love reveals itself in holy self-sacrifice: **'In this the love of God was manifested toward us, that God has sent his only begotten Son into the world, that we might live through him. In this is love, not that we loved God, but that he loved us and sent his Son to be the propitiation for our sins'** (4:9-10). The love of God manifested itself not only in the sending of his Son to this earth for thirty years, but in his coming to die. The Son of God died on the cross as the propitiation (not the RSV's 'expiation' or even just the NIV's 'atoning sacrifice'[5]) for our sins. He died to satisfy God's own justice.

God was looking at sinners who were all going their own way to hell. He loved them, but he could not save them without his justice being satisfied. He said, 'I love my people, my elect, my chosen ones, my sheep, my bride. They have trampled on my law; they have lived selfish lives and been guilty of all kinds of sin before me. But I will send my Son to bear their punishment. Then I will have nothing against them. Then I can love them with justice and mercy.'

It is not that Christ won the love of the Father for his people, but that the Father in love sent Christ to be the propitiation for our sins. Christ became the propitiation for the sins of the unlovely — for those who are ungodly (Rom. 5:6), who are sinners (Rom. 5:8) and who are his enemies (Rom. 5:10). God sought our good at great cost to himself. God was not responding to our love; God is the origin of our love. God's free grace is costly — it cost him his beloved Son and it will cost us our sin. God's love does not ignore sin but endures hell for sinners. At Calvary God's mercy and righteousness met together in perfect harmony. His holy wrath was poured out upon his Son, so sinners can be justified through faith in him (Rom. 3:25-26).

The love of the Christian

If we profess to believe in Christ, a proof that this profession is genuine is that we love the people of Christ. **'Beloved, let us love one another, for love is of God; and everyone who loves is born of God and knows God'** (4:7). **'And we have known and believed the love that God has for us. God is love, and he who abides in love abides in God, and God in him'** (4:16). Since the Christian knows the gracious love of God, he cannot say, 'I am unable to love my wife because she is cold towards me and annoys me,' or 'I cannot love this or that person because he snubbed me in the street.' One of the evidences that we are born again is love towards our Christian brothers and sisters. Such love comes from God, and shows that **'He has given us of his Spirit'** (4:13). Because of the work of the Spirit, the love of God mentioned in verses 9 and 16 is not merely 'towards us' or 'for us', but, to be literal, 'in us'. As is often pointed out, love is the first of the nine manifestations of the fruit of the Spirit (Gal. 5:22-23). This love is no more earned than our salvation is. It is gracious and self-giving, while not ignoring sin and the claims of holy justice.

The Christian's love for his fellow Christians — of whatever denomination, social status or race — is something that flows from the love of God. **'Beloved, if God so loved us, we also ought to love one another'** (4:11). It is not just *a* proof that we are born again but a *necessary* proof: **'If someone says, "I love God," and hates his brother, he is a liar; for he who does not love his brother whom he has seen, how can he love God whom he has not seen? And this commandment we have from him: that he who loves God must love his brother also'** (4:20-21).⁶ The man who professes to be a Christian but ruthlessly makes his Christian brother look small at work is showing the unregenerate state of his heart. The woman who takes the name of 'Christian' but cannot wait to gossip about her Christian neighbour gives herself away. We cannot bless God and curse men and women who have been made in the likeness of God (James 3:9).

'Hatred' may not take the form of overt viciousness. It may simply mean our natural love of ourselves, which shows itself in self-centredness, self-assertion, self-pity, self-indulgence, self-seeking, or self-righteousness. As John Newton lamented, 'I have read of many wicked popes, but the worst pope I ever met with is Pope Self.'⁷ To love someone does not require us to agree with him or her at all times, but to seek the welfare of the other person even at cost to ourselves. Love that is a reflection of God's love draws us out of ourselves. How does your life measure up to these exacting standards?

The Christian's love for God

John says, **'Love has been perfected among us in this: that we may have boldness in the day of judgement; because as he is, so are we in this world. There is no fear in love;**

but perfect love casts out fear, because fear involves torment. But he who fears has not been made perfect in love' (4:17-18). These are verses that can be much misunderstood — in fact, 1 John can be a dangerous book to use for proof-texts.[8] For the person outside of Christ, the problem is often not too much fear of God but not enough. This is Paul's point in Romans 3:18, where he quotes from Psalm 36:1: 'There is no fear of God before their eyes.' It was the lack of such fear in Gerar that led Abraham to try to pass off his wife Sarah as his sister (Gen. 20:11). Abraham thought that the king might kill him and take Sarah — who was ageing but still good-looking — into his harem. Even for the Christian, saved by grace and destined for glory, there is a sense in which he is to fear God (see Eph. 5:21; 1 Peter 1:17).

John is not abolishing that kind of fear, but is referring to a Christian's maturing love for God. As this love grows and develops, the Christian grows in boldness and assurance (see also 2:28). As Calvin says, the love of God 'tranquillizes the heart', and Christians can go to God's tribunal 'confidently and cheerfully, because they feel assured of his paternal love'.[9] As love is perfected, the servile fear of torment recedes into the background. Literally, John says that love 'throws away' fear. The Christian knows that Christ has already borne his or her punishment (John 3:18). This takes away the fear of death and judgement which was there before the Christian turned to Christ. To illustrate this, if a man loves his wife, he does not refuse to commit adultery because he fears that God, or his wife, will punish him. Higher motives are at work. As love is made complete, it casts out fear.

The basis for this is not a weak view of God. A most immoral woman once complained to me in the street while it was pouring with rain, 'What is God doing? We do not deserve this!' The Christian answer is: 'No, madam, we do not. We deserve to be wiped off the face of the earth by a flood as in Noah's day.' Calvin maintained that 'By nature, indeed, we dread the presence of God, and that justly; for, as he is the Judge of the world, and our sins hold us guilty, death and hell must come to our minds whenever we think of God.'[10] That is probably true if we probe deeply enough, but, on the surface at least, it seems today that complacency casts out fear.

The Bible maintains a balance in all this. 'It is a fearful thing to fall into the hands of the living God' (Heb. 10:31). Yet the same book exhorts us: 'Let us therefore come boldly to the throne of grace, that we may obtain mercy and find grace to help in time of need' (Heb. 4:16). Dare we approach *boldly* one who is a consuming fire, whom we are told to fear?

> That day of wrath, that dreadful day,
> When heaven and earth shall pass away,
> What power shall be the sinner's stay?
> How shall he meet that dreadful day?
>
> (Walter Scott)

Yet the Bible says we can approach that day with a reverent boldness, for we have a great High Priest who has passed through the heavens, Jesus the Son of God, one who is sinless and majestic in all holiness, but one who has been tempted and can sympathize with us in all our weaknesses (see Heb. 2:17-18; 4:14-15). Hence Charles Wesley could sing:

> Bold I approach the eternal throne,
> And claim the crown, through Christ my own.

Love had cast out Charles Wesley's fear; it is the unbeliever who lives in the bondage of the fear of death (Heb. 2:15). There is an element of paradox in the Christian's approach to God. F. W. Faber captures this in his hymn:

When most I fear thee, Lord, then most
Familiar I appear;
And I am in my soul most free,
When I am most in fear.

Robert Candlish put it like this: 'Love; the holy love of God; of the Father sending the Son to be the Saviour of the world; is now the habitual home of our hearts.'[11]

But perhaps the last word should belong to poetry rather than prose. Hence the words of Horatius Bonar:

Beloved, let us love:
Love is of God;
In God alone hath love
Its true abode.

Beloved, let us love:
For they who love,
They only, are his sons,
Born from above...

Beloved, let us love:
For only thus
Shall we behold that God
Who loveth us.

13.
Summarizing the three tests

Please read 1 John 5:1-5

John is now moving towards the conclusion of his epistle, and he draws together these three tests that are set before every Christian — faith in Jesus Christ as the Son of God, love for his people and obedience to his commandments.

The rebirth comes first

John has made this clear all through his epistle (see, for example, 3:9; 4:7). Now he raises the issue again: **'Whoever believes that Jesus is the Christ is born of God, and everyone who loves him who begot also loves him who is begotten of him'** (5:1). The use in the Greek of the perfect tense needs to be brought out more clearly: 'Whoever believes [present tense] that Jesus is the Christ has been born [perfect tense] of God.' The perfect tense is used when something which occurred in the past has an abiding influence into the future. In this case, the rebirth brought about by the Holy Spirit leads to faith in Jesus as the Christ.

Billy Graham once wrote a book entitled *How to be Born Again* in which he treated regeneration as being the same as conversion. Most evangelists from the latter part of the nineteenth century and into the twentieth century have taught that when we come to Christ by faith, we are born again by the Spirit of God. This is not the case; it is the other way around. The Spirit comes to sinners who are spiritually dead (John 5:24-25; Eph. 2:1-6), wilfully ignorant (Eph. 4:18), bound in sin (John 8:34) and alienated from God (Col. 1:21), and he makes them spiritually alive, enlightened, free and reconciled in Christ. In regeneration the principle of new life is implanted in the sinner, and the governing disposition of the soul is now that of holiness before a holy God. This is not something we can achieve for ourselves, or even decide to let God achieve for us. Spiritual life must come from God first before we can trust in Christ and pass these three tests about which John has been writing.

If our faith is true, it must come from the Holy Spirit, the Lord and giver of life. To quote the Puritan John Preston, 'A woman many times thinks she is with child, but if she finds no motion or stirring, it is an argument she was deceived. So, when a man thinks he has faith in his heart, but yet he finds no life, no motion, no stirring, there is no work proceeding from his faith, it is an argument he was mistaken, he was deceived in it: for if it be a right faith, it will work, there will be life and motion in it.'[1]

The biblical message is that true, Spirit-given faith has life, and so it works (Gal. 5:6; James 2:14-26).

The three proofs are interconnected

In verse 1 John joins the belief test to the love test: **'Whoever believes that Jesus is the Christ is born of God, and everyone who loves him who begot also loves him who is begotten of him'** (5:1). In his letter to the Colossians, Paul mentions that he gave thanks to God and prayed for the Colossian Christians 'since we heard of your faith in Christ Jesus and of your love for all the saints' (Col. 1:3-4). The Christians at Colosse passed these two of John's tests — they possessed faith and love. But John is quick to mention the test of obedience: **'By this we know that we love the children of God, when we love God and keep his commandments'** (5:2). That sounds a little strange to us — a test for knowing whether you love Christians is 'Do you love God and obey his commandments?' John is making it clear just how interconnected the three tests are.

A Christian is one who has faith in Jesus as the Christ (5:1) and the Son of God (5:5). Such a person loves those who share the same faith and seek to keep God's commandments. Jesus said, 'If you love me, keep my commandments' (John 14:15). **'For this is the love of God, that we keep his commandments'** (5:3). If a coin had three sides, we might say that faith, love and obedience are three sides to the one coin! Perhaps we should say that they are like three threads in the one fabric. They can be distinguished but they cannot be separated in the life of the Christian.

It is wrong to say, 'What matters is that we all love one another. Doctrine is irrelevant.' That is separating what John unites. Similarly, when someone says, 'We need to get back to some good old-fashioned morality and teach our youngsters to obey God's laws,' that is only one-third of the whole story. Someone else might say, 'What we need in our church is sound doctrine. No more liberalism and no more Arminianism!' True enough, but sound doctrine had better go hand-in-hand with love and obedience or the result will be most unlovely. If we have been born of the Holy Spirit, we will have a right belief in Jesus Christ for our salvation, a love for all our fellow Christians and a hunger to obey God's commandments. These three things need to be found in us for us to have any assurance that we truly belong to Christ.

God's easy yoke

The world's perception of God's commandments is a major problem today, but it has always been so: **'For this is the love of God, that we keep his commandments. And his commandments are not burdensome'** (5:3). To the unregenerate, there is freedom in doing what one likes, and the commandments of God are seen as a burden and an irritation. Indeed, they are positively irksome. 'Not so,' says our Lord. 'Come to me, all you who labour and are heavy laden, and I will give you rest. Take my yoke upon you and learn from me, for I am gentle and lowly in heart, and you will find rest for your souls. For my yoke is easy and my burden is light' (Matt. 11:28-30) — a contrast to the Pharisaic approach in Matthew 23:4.

The world's perception is tragically jaundiced. God's way is not a burden; it is sin's way that proves to be burdensome. God tells children, 'Honour your father and mother,' but the world says, 'Do your own thing.' We need to ask ourselves, 'Have the burdens in our lives come from obeying God or from disobeying him?' We see hassled mothers everywhere because their children are unruly. Even getting ready for church can become a major operation. Children do not readily obey, so everything takes longer to complete, and the stress level is increased in the meantime.

You will find that this is true of all the commandments. Where is the burden in the home when husband and wife love each other with consideration and fidelity? Where is the burden at work where there is honesty, diligence and trust? Where is the burden at the supermarket where there is a mutual concern to serve one another? It is our sins that are burdensome, as John Bunyan portrayed so graphically in *Pilgrim's Progress*. Selfishness, dishonesty, covetousness, drunkenness, idolatry, pride and lust will weigh us down if we give in to them; serving

Christ will set us free. The unbeliever maintains that Christianity is a burden — it consists of commands: 'Don't do this and don't do that'. It is stifling and restrictive. In thinking this way, the unbeliever fails to see that God's laws are designed for our benefit. Sin is an offence against the majesty of God, but it is also a burden to sinners.

Obeying God will land us in trouble with the world. Jeremiah found that he did not sit in the assembly of the mockers but had to sit alone because of his God-given indignation at Judah's sin (Jer. 15:17). The apostle Peter warns Christians that unbelievers will think it strange that we do not run with them in 'lewdness, lusts, drunkenness, revelries, drinking parties, and abominable idolatries', and they will speak evil of us (1 Peter 4:3-4). But Jeremiah still declared to God:

> Your words were found, and I ate them,
> And your word was to me the joy and rejoicing of my
>   heart;
> For I am called by your name,
> O Lord God of hosts
>
> (Jer. 15:16).

Peter too writes of being born again through the word of God (1 Peter 1:23) and rejoicing with 'joy inexpressible and full of glory' (1 Peter 1:8). God's commandments may lead to some grief for God's people in this fallen world, but ultimately there is delight. Sin may bring some passing pleasure for a time, but ultimately there will be misery.

The victory of faith

The rebirth ushers in victory for the Christian: **'For whatever is born of God overcomes the world. And this is the victory**

that has overcome the world — our faith' (5:4). What can touch the Christian? Sin? Yes, but Christ has paid the penalty for sin. Sickness? Yes, but Christ has power to heal if he so chooses. Death? Yes, but Christ has overcome death. Satan? Yes, but he is a defeated foe for 'He who is in you is greater than he who is in the world' (4:4). Hell? No, for Christ has endured the equivalent of hell on behalf of his people. 'Yet in all these things we are more than conquerors through him who loved us. For I am persuaded that neither death nor life, nor angels nor principalities nor powers, nor things present nor things to come, nor height nor depth, nor any other created thing, shall be able to separate us from the love of God which is in Christ Jesus our Lord' (Rom. 8:37-39). Christ has overcome all these things, and he is the victor. His victory will be shared with all who have faith in him. Faith gives us victory because it joins us to Christ, who has won the victory over the world, the flesh and the devil.

During the Reformation in England, John Hooper was consecrated Bishop of Gloucester in 1551. Things turned ominous for the Protestants when Mary Tudor came to the throne in 1553. By 1555 the burnings had begun, and soon Hooper, as an evangelical, was sentenced to be burnt at the stake. While he was in prison, Hooper was visited by one of his friends, Sir Anthony Kingston, who urged him to recant and go back to the Roman Catholic faith. Kingston pleaded with much affection and with many tears, 'Consider that life is sweet, and death is bitter.' To which Hooper replied, 'The life to come is more sweet, and the death to come is more bitter.'[2] So it was that on 9 February 1555 Hooper was burnt at the stake.

Yet it was not defeat but victory: 'Then I heard a loud voice saying in heaven, "Now salvation, and strength, and the kingdom of our God, and the power of his Christ have come, for the accuser of our brethren, who accused them before our God day and night, has been cast down. And they overcame him by the blood of the Lamb and by the word of their testimony, and they did not love their lives to the death" ' (Rev. 12:10-11). There is victory, even in death:

> Hell is nigh, but God is nigher,
> Circling us with hosts of fire.
>
> (Charles Wesley)

The proof of our rebirth is not spectacular gifts nor wondrous doings. It is right belief, love and obedience — all together. This will not be a burden at all, but joy and light, for the promise is for victory through faith in Christ.

14.
Belief and unbelief

Please read 1 John 5:6-12

Here John presses home the issue of faith and unbelief. He does this by pointing to the testimonies to the truth of the gospel. The Greek word for 'testify' or 'bear witness' occurs ten times in 1 John 5:6-11. John is showing that the testimony to Christ is so strong that we have no reason for rejecting it.

The three witnesses

It needs to be said at the outset that the manuscript support for verse 7 and the first part of verse 8 — concerning the heavenly witness of the Father, the Word and the Holy Spirit — is very weak. The teaching is biblical — God is triune (three persons in one), as the baptismal formula makes clear (Matt. 28:19). However, the passage from 1 John about the three heavenly witnesses is only found in a few late Greek manuscripts, and was almost certainly added by some Trinitarians rather than removed by some Arians (those who denied the doctrine of the Trinity) — despite Robert Lewis Dabney's valiant attempt to rescue it.[1] What the text does say is that there are three witnesses — the water, the blood and the Spirit — and these three witnesses agree in testifying to the truth of Jesus Christ. The law demands that 'By the mouth of two or three witnesses the matter shall be established' (Deut. 19:15).

We can understand why there are three witnesses, but what does John mean by the water, the blood and the Spirit? Martin Luther claimed that the water is baptism and the blood is the Lord's Supper, but that seems most unlikely.[2] Apart from anything else, blood only symbolizes half of the Lord's Supper. Robert Candlish seems to combine a number of views. He begins by pointing, as Augustine did, to the cross, and the blood and water which flowed from Jesus' side when it was pierced by the soldier's spear (John 19:34-35). But then he goes on to write in Levitical terms of the water as cleansing and the blood as atoning.[3] James Montgomery Boice thinks that it is 'not impossible' that water symbolizes the Scripture,[4] but this seems even more strained than Luther's interpretation.

The best suggestion seems to be that the water refers to Jesus' baptism while the blood refers to his death.[5] The reality of the passion points to the reality of the incarnation. The whole public ministry of Jesus — from his baptism to his crucifixion — shows that the Christ had come in the flesh. This was the pivotal point which Cerinthus and his fellow heretics denied.[6] Ultimately, the whole public ministry of Christ testifies to the truth of his person and work. In fact, Christ is testified to by God the Father (John 5:32,37), the Holy Spirit (John 15:26), John the Baptist (John 1:15; 5:33), Christ's own works (John 5:36; 10:25), the Scriptures (John 5:39), the disciples (John 15:27) and the crowds of people who saw what the Lord did (John 12:17).

The Spirit is the internal witness. He testifies with the water and the blood. Jesus had prophesied, 'But when the Helper *[Parakletos]* comes, whom I shall send to you from the Father, the Spirit of truth who proceeds from the Father, he will testify of me' (John 15:26). We have the outward evidence of Christ — his life, his teachings, his compassion, his miracles, his death and resurrection. But without the inward testimony of the Spirit, we would not believe these things; they would remain foreign to us. One person hears of Christ and is moved and convicted by the Spirit — he knows no peace until he rests upon Christ by faith. Another person hears the same message and can hardly wait till it finishes and he can go home to turn on the television or go to the beach.

The nineteenth-century evangelical politician and campaigner against slavery, William Wilberforce, once brought his friend William Pitt (the youngest man ever to be Prime Minister of Britain) to hear Richard Cecil preach. Cecil proclaimed the gospel and Wilberforce revelled in it, feeling he was almost in heaven. At the conclusion of the service he could hardly wait to ask Pitt what he made of it. Pitt was an intelligent man but not an evangelical, and he could only reply, 'I didn't understand a word of what that man was talking about. What was it?'[7] The Spirit of God was testifying to Wilberforce but not to Pitt. As Charles Wesley put it,

> His Spirit answers to the blood,
> And tells me I am born of God.

Do you have this testimony? Do the water, the blood and the Spirit bear witness to you and in you that Christ is your sin-bearer, that he has borne God's wrath in your place?

The response to the testimony

John argues quite simply, **'If we receive the witness of men, the witness of God is greater; for this is the witness of God which he has testified of his Son. He who believes in the Son of God has the witness in himself; he who does not believe God has made him a liar, because he has not believed the testimony that God has given of his Son'** (5:9-10). Verse 9 is saying what is generally true: we accept human testimony, so we ought to accept the testimony of God, which is greater. Some time back I recall being with about fifteen other parents from our local Christian school. One parent commented on a *Peter and the Wolf* show which our children had seen in a nearby country centre. I corrected this parent, and said that the children had indeed seen *Peter and the Wolf*, but at another country centre. Eventually, all the parents became involved in our conversation, and they all sided with the other parent, not me. I persisted for a short while, but had to admit I must have been wrong. Later I found out that I was! One of my children had gone to the centre that I had mentioned, and I wrongly assumed that all the other students had done the same. It is usually reasonable to accept human testimony as true.

Surely, then, it is far more reasonable to accept that God's testimony is true. The Father's testimony to the Son was heard at Jesus' baptism: 'When he had been baptized, Jesus came up immediately from the water; and behold, the heavens were opened to him, and he saw the Spirit of God descending like a dove and alighting upon him. And suddenly a voice came from heaven, saying, "This is my beloved Son, in whom I am well pleased" ' (Matt. 3:16-17). It was heard again when Jesus was transfigured: 'While he was still speaking, behold, a bright cloud overshadowed them; and suddenly a voice came out of the cloud, saying, "This is my beloved Son, in whom I am well pleased. Hear him!" ' (Matt. 17:5). Just before the crucifixion, Jesus prayed, 'Now my soul is troubled, and what shall I say? "Father, save me from this hour?" But for this purpose I came to this hour. Father, glorify your name.' The response came with the divine voice from heaven: 'I have both glorified it and will glorify it again' (John 12:27-28).

What are you saying if you reject this testimony? Verse 10 says that you would be calling God a liar! The Father testifies to the truth of Christ, but the unbeliever dismisses it as not worth his time in investigating. To cite John Stott, 'Unbelief is not a misfortune to be pitied; it is a sin to be deplored.'[8] The person without the Holy Spirit may concede that gang rape is sinful but he does not think of unbelief as a sin. But behind unbelief is a rebellious and sinful unwillingness to investigate the claims of Christ. The Father declares, 'This is my beloved Son. He is true.' But the sinner says, 'So what! Other things are more important in my life.' He may do that in an erudite and sophisticated way, as Bertrand Russell did in his collection of essays entitled *Why I Am Not a Christian.*[9] God does not regard that as simply Russell's opinion to which he was entitled. It was sin — Russell was calling God a liar. We must not pander to sinful unbelief.

God's concluding testimony

John is straightforward enough in his conclusion: **'And this is the testimony: that God has given us eternal life, and this life is in his Son. He who has the Son has life; he who does not have the Son of God does not have life'** (5:11-12). We surely cannot misunderstand such a clear statement about the spiritual condition of all humanity on this earth. As has been said, either we know Christ and so know life, or for us there is no Christ and so no life. Each of us is either enjoying life in all its wondrous abundance, or enduring death in all its horrific abundance (note John 10:10). It is no good thinking that we have made a success of our lives if we do not have Christ. It is no good thinking that we are decent people if Christ has not redeemed us. Christianity is Christ. Either he is ours and we are his, or everlasting death is ours for ever.

Each of the verbs in verse 12 is in the present tense: **'He who has the Son** [i.e. repents of sin and trusts in Christ alone at this very moment] **has life** [i.e. is even now possessing that life which will be perfectly righteous for all eternity]; **he who does not have the Son of God** [i.e. is believing in someone or something else for his salvation] **does not have life** [i.e. is damned now and will be for ever unless he repents].' Or, to quote John 3:18, 'He who believes in him [Christ] is not condemned; but he who does not believe is condemned already, because he has not believed in the name of the only begotten Son of God.' Your death may be years away, even decades away, and the day of Christ's coming again may not be for centuries. But you can know your standing before God now. This verse tells you where you are before Almighty God.

God has given many witnesses to Christ — the water, the blood and the Spirit. We usually accept man's testimony, so we have greater reason to accept God's testimony. Not to do so is to call God a liar. His testimony is the final word on the subject.

15.
Assurance in the Christian life

Please read 1 John 5:13-17

John tells us that he wrote his Gospel so that people might believe in the Lord Jesus Christ: 'And truly Jesus did many other signs in the presence of his disciples, which are not written in this book; but these are written that you may believe that Jesus is the Christ, the Son of God, and that believing you may have life in his name' (John 20:30-31). He wrote his first epistle, however, to professing Christians, to people who had already placed their trust in Christ: **'These things I have written to you who believe in the name of the Son of God, that you may know that you have eternal life [and that you may continue to believe in the name of the Son of God]'** (5:13).[1] This naturally raises the whole issue of assurance in the Christian life. Can we be assured that we belong to God?

The doctrine of assurance

John has written to those 'who believe in the name of the Son of God' that they might press on to the next stage and 'know that [they] have eternal life' (5:13). Many churches and virtually all the cults teach that assurance is not possible. In replying to the Protestant Reformation, the Roman Catholic Council of Trent (which met in three sessions from 1545 to 1564)

declared in 1547 in its *Decrees concerning Justification* that
'Except by special revelation, it cannot be known whom God
has chosen to himself.'[2] Furthermore, 'If anyone says that he
will for certain, with an absolute and infallible certainty, have
that great gift of perseverance even to the end, unless he shall
have learned this by a special revelation, let him be anath-
ema.'[3] By 'special revelation', the Council of Trent was not
referring to the Scriptures but to a dream or a vision given to
a special individual. Hence, Cardinal Bellarmine denounced
the Reformation doctrine of assurance as 'a prime error of
heretics'. The apostle John, in contrast, wrote to ordinary Christians, seeking to give them assurance that they could *know*
that they possessed eternal life in Christ. Assurance is not 'a
prime error of heretics' but a clear teaching of Scripture. The
Christian can indeed know that nothing in time or eternity can
separate him from the love of God in Christ Jesus (Rom.
8:28-39).

Yet it is true that there is such a thing as presumption. People
can think they are Christians — they may even feel certain
that they are Christians — when they are nothing of the kind.
To the unruly Corinthians, Paul wrote, 'Examine yourselves
as to whether you are in the faith. Test yourselves. Do you not
know yourselves, that Jesus Christ is in you? — unless indeed
you are disqualified' (2 Cor. 13:5). John himself has been es-
tablishing three tests to apply to those who claim to be Christians. Do we believe in Jesus as the Christ, the God-man? Do
we love those who also believe in him? Do we seek to keep
the Lord's commandments? If we fail those three tests and
still claim assurance, we are deluding ourselves, we are guilty
of presumption.

Verse 13, however, is dealing with assurance, not presumption. If you are truly a Christian, one of the consequences of
working through John's first epistle (or any portion of God's
Word, for that matter) is that you should grow in your

assurance. The worst thing the church can do for non-Christians is to convince them that they are Christians; the best thing it can do for true Christians is to assure them of God's electing and everlasting love.

A grasp of assurance will not cause us to put our feet up and rest. On the contrary, assurance will enliven us to press on with greater labours in the kingdom. If I am not sure that I own a piece of property, I will not do much to improve it. Why work too hard for what may not be mine? But if I am certain that I possess the title deeds, then I will be keen to do all I can to make it what it ought to be. It is the same in the Christian life. Presumption and doubt put the sinner to sleep; faith and assurance animate the believer to greater godliness.

Assurance in prayer

John applies the doctrine of assurance to the prayer life of the Christian in verses 14-15: **'Now this is the confidence that we have in him, that if we ask anything according to his will, he hears us. And if we know that he hears us, whatever we ask, we know that we have the petitions that we have asked of him.'** We often fail here; we are too timid. I have met people in trouble who try out prayer along with a lot of other things in the hope that one of them might work. That is a poor way to approach God. The Christian should keep the precious truths of the Bible in mind as he prays: 'For we do not have a High Priest who cannot sympathize with our weaknesses, but was in all points tempted as we are, yet without sin. Let us therefore come boldly to the throne of grace, that we may obtain mercy and find grace to help in time of need' (Heb. 4:15-16). If we trust someone, we speak to that person confidently because we believe that he or she wants the best for us. It is the same with God. We trust his Word, we trust his character, we trust his motives — hence we are both reverent and confident before him.

There is just one condition: 'according to his will' (5:14). The Word of Faith movement denies this condition and Gloria Copeland, for example, asserts that ' "If it be thy will" is unbelief when praying for healing.'[4] Colin Urquhart even calls it a 'faith-killing statement'.[5] But prayer is not a blank cheque to write in whatever takes our fancy. One children's catechism asks, 'What is prayer?' The answer is: 'Prayer is asking God for things which he has promised to give.' Can we boldly ask God for our daily bread? Yes, we can, for he tells us to do so (Ps. 37:25; Matt. 6:11; Phil. 4:19). Can we boldly ask him that we might win the lottery? No, because he tells us to be content with what we have and not to covet (Exod. 20:17; Phil. 4:11-12). But what if we promise to give the winnings to missions? The answer is still 'No' because the ends do not justify the means (Rom. 3:8). It is a mockery to pray against God's revealed will. There is no point in praying for the dead. Nor can a husband pray whether to leave his wife and take up with another woman. Nor can a woman pray whether she should become a pastor. God has spoken on these issues, and it is futile and dishonouring to God to pray against his will.

In a situation where we cannot know God's will with certainty — for example, when we are praying for someone with a terminal illness — we can pray for that person's recovery, in confidence that nothing is too hard for the Lord, but also in submission that his will may be done. Even if God refuses our request, it is because of his goodness and his concern for our eternal welfare. Earthly fathers, if they have any idea of what fatherhood is about, will not agree to every request from their youngsters. The father who agrees to endless pleas for ice creams, toys and holidays will soon prove to be an ineffective parent who is doing more harm than good. For all that, the Christian can approach God's throne with a holy boldness.

The leader of the 1843 Disruption in Scotland, Thomas Chalmers, once wrote in his diary, 'Make me sensible of real answers to actual requests, as evidences of an interchange between myself on earth and my Saviour in heaven.' He was seeking to grow in assurance as he came to God in prayer; he wanted to know that his prayers were making a difference in human history.

Prayer and sin

Perhaps surprisingly, John says that there is an exception to our boldness in prayer. This exception has to do with a certain kind of sin. **'If anyone sees his brother sinning a sin which does not lead to death, he will ask, and he will give him life for those who commit sin not leading to death. There is sin leading to death. I do not say that he should pray about that. All unrighteousness is sin, and there is sin not leading to death'** (5:16-17). This presupposes that if we see a Christian slipping away from the Lord, we will not gossip about the person but pray that he will be restored (see James 5:20). Yet the apostle John does not encourage prayer for a sinner whose sin leads to death. We might be tempted to respond that it is surely Christian to pray for everybody. That, however, is not so. We often hear today that God's love is boundless, but that is a notion which belongs to the New Age movement, not to the Christian church. The God of the Bible may well give up on a people who have turned their backs on him. Before the destruction of Jerusalem by the Babylonians in 587 B.C., Jeremiah was told, 'Therefore do not pray for this people, nor lift up a cry or prayer for them, nor make intercession to me; for I will not hear you' (Jer. 7:16).

Back will come the objection, as it does from C. H. Dodd: 'This is not very Christ-like.'[6] Yet in his prayer on the night before his crucifixion, Christ specifically declared to his Father, 'I pray for them. I do not pray for the world but for those whom you have given me, for they are yours' (John 17:9). He also stated that there are times when we should not indiscriminately present the gospel to people: 'Do not give what is holy to the dogs; nor cast your pearls before swine, lest they trample them under their feet, and turn and tear you in pieces' (Matt. 7:6). It is true that normally we should be encouraging Christians to present the gospel to their friends and neighbours, but there are rare times when it is right to withhold the gospel. I can only recall using this verse once, to a married man who wanted me to save his marriage but refused to give up his girlfriend. After repeated entreaties were refused, I finally quoted this verse to him, and ended the counselling session. Interestingly enough, this episode had a happy ending although I played no part in its final outcome. This whole concept is a difficult one to apply in a pastoral situation, but one can only assume that John had in mind Christ's teaching on the blasphemy against the Holy Spirit which is subject to eternal condemnation. This is the sin of believing that Christ is possessed of an unclean spirit (Mark 3:28-30).

Some of the Fathers of the early church believed that John was referring to major sins like murder, adultery and idolatry. This does not seem to fit in with other portions of Scripture. Christ prayed for Peter, who was to deny him three times: 'And the Lord said, "Simon, Simon! Indeed, Satan has asked for you, that he may sift you as wheat. But I have prayed for you, that your faith should not fail; and when you have returned to me, strengthen your brethren" ' (Luke 22:31-32). That ought to encourage us to pray earnestly if we see someone slipping away from Christ. Yet it is also said that God gives up on certain people (Rom. 1:24,26,28). 'God is not mocked' (Gal. 6:7). There are people who may become so hard-hearted that Christians should refuse to give them the gospel or even to pray for them. In the 1930s, for example, the Lutheran theologian, Dietrich Bonhoeffer, came to the conclusion that it was pointless for Frank Buchman and the Oxford Group in England to pray for the conversion of Adolf Hitler. In a letter in 1934 Bonhoeffer complained: 'The Oxford Movement has been naïve enough to try to convert Hitler — a ridiculous failure to understand what is going on...'[7] We need to be careful in such matters — after all, Manasseh was converted after a lifetime of idolatry and brutality, including even child sacrifice (2 Chron. 33:1-17). But Scripture makes it plain that a situation may indeed come about where the gospel is *not* presented to someone.

John is specifically referring to a professing brother — a confessed Christian — who commits the sin leading to death. Some of the fiercest opponents of biblical Christianity have at one time been professing believers. The Gnostics of John's day started out as those who once claimed to have been converted to Christ Jesus. But if we are doubtful about whether we should continue to witness to a person and pray for him or her, we should persevere. We must always err on the side of charity.

16.
Knowing where we stand

Please read 1 John 5:18-21

1 John is an epistle about testing a Christian profession — by right doctrine, by love and by obedience to the commandments. Hence it is also an epistle about assurance — we can know that we know. Not all Christianity that is presented in the form of dogma is true Christianity, but true Christianity by its nature involves dogma, or in other words, a system of doctrine. As Martin Luther informed Erasmus in their debate at the time of the Reformation over the bondage of the human will, 'Take away assertions, and you take away Christianity.'[1] The apostle John writes in a similar vein. He is not tentatively suggesting a few hypotheses. He is making clear affirmations: 'We know...' (5:18); 'We know...' (5:19), 'And we know...' (5:20). That is the language of biblical Christianity. We are to be humble about ourselves but confident about what God has revealed. John finishes off his first epistle with three affirmations and one warning.

An affirmation about holiness

John declares, **'We know that whoever is born of God does not sin; but he who has been born of God keeps himself, and the wicked one does not touch him'** (5:18). This ought to be a ringing affirmation with us — the Christian is not given over to sin. The Christian sins — we recall what John said earlier about any claim to sinless perfection (1:8,10) — but he is not a prisoner of sin. 'No one who is born of God will continue to sin' (3:9, NIV). A person who entrenches himself in serious sin is outside the kingdom of God. The new birth results in new behaviour. Sin cannot be habitual for the Christian.

The NIV, RSV and most other translations say that Jesus, the one who is born of God, keeps the Christian. Praise God, Christ does sustain us and gives us strength to persevere. Our Lord himself declares, 'This is the will of the Father who sent me, that of all he has given me I should lose nothing, but should raise it up at the last day' (John 6:39). Also he prayed, 'While I was with them in the world, I kept them in your name. Those whom you gave me I have kept; and none of them is lost except the son of perdition, that the Scripture might be fulfilled' (John 17:12). It is thus true that Christ keeps his people.

Yet the NKJV may still be correct in translating the passage to mean that the Christian, as one who has been born of God, keeps himself. The notion of a Christian's keeping himself or herself is not in itself Arminian, nor is it necessarily a recipe for despair, as David Jackman thinks.[2] It is found elsewhere in Scripture: 'Keep yourself pure' (1 Tim. 5:22), '... keep oneself unspotted from the world' (James 1:27); 'Keep yourselves in the love of God' (Jude 21). Sanctification, like justification, is a work of God's free grace. But God works in us to make us active. The understanding of sanctification traditionally associated with the Keswick Convention — whereby we simply receive it by faith — is defective and unfaithful to Scripture.[3] However true it is that Christ keeps his people, it is also true that the Christian maintains his own walk before God.

John does not say that the Christian *should* keep himself, but takes it as given that he does keep himself. A Christian is by definition serious about killing sin in his life — dealing with the bad old habits of indiscipline, correcting the way he speaks to members of his family, controlling the worldly considerations which so easily crowd out our concern for spiritual reality. The wicked one does not 'touch', or cling to, the Christian. The Christian may fall into sin but it does not become a way of life for him. The Christian *knows* that the devil has been bound. He also *knows* that holiness is not an optional extra in the Christian life.

An affirmation about where we stand

John's second affirmation is: **'We know that we are of God, and the whole world lies under the sway of the wicked one'** (5:19). One of the most dreadful things about the life of the non-Christian is that he is often oblivious to the danger that he faces. The whole world is under the power (RSV), or control (NIV), of the evil one. This does not mean that God is not sovereign. 'Our God is in heaven,' says the psalmist. 'He does whatever he pleases' (Ps. 115:3). He laughs with derision at those who seek to rebel against his rule and the rule of his Anointed (Ps. 2:4). Nevertheless, Satan does possess real, even though not final, power. Most of the world, however, does not even realize that, let alone escape it.

In recent times in the Western world there has been an increase in the level of activity to do with the occult. Most bookshops now carry far more literature dealing with the occult than with orthodox Christianity. Sometimes the devil himself is openly worshipped and, associated with this, there may be human sacrifice, sadism and the most degraded promiscuity. Most non-Christians, however, do not consciously adore his infernal majesty. They seem oblivious to spiritual realities. As Paul says, 'But even if our gospel is veiled, it is veiled to those who are perishing, whose minds the god of this age has blinded, who do not believe, lest the light of the gospel of the glory of Christ, who is the image of God, should shine on them' (2 Cor. 4:3-4). Such people are under Satan's sway, but they do not know it. In fact, if you were to tell them this, they would laugh at you and think that you were joking. Only the Christian knows the true state of affairs. There are only two categories of people — those who belong to God and those who belong to Satan. The Christian is thankful that he knows where he stands.

An affirmation about the truth in Christ

John's third affirmation is: **'And we know that the Son of God has come and has given us an understanding, that we may know him who is true; and we are in him who is true, in his Son Jesus Christ. This is the true God and eternal life'** (5:20). This is clearly the most fundamental affirmation. The Son of God has come to earth from heaven; the Lord of glory has descended to this sick and sorry world. This is the truth of the incarnation: 'For you know the grace of our Lord Jesus Christ, that though he was rich, yet for your sakes he became poor, that you through his poverty might become rich' (2 Cor. 8:9). This is not something about which the Christian should have any doubts.

Nor should the Christian have any doubts about his or her faith in Christ. The Christian knows that the Son has come to this earth, and he knows that God has given us the capacity to believe in him. Faith is exercised by us, but it is given by God — or, as here, by the Son of God (5:20). Our Lord said the same thing: 'All things have been delivered to me by my Father, and no one knows the Son except the Father. Nor does anyone know the Father except the Son, and the one to whom the Son wills to reveal him' (Matt. 11:27). Christ gives the gift of faith. One person hears, yet does not hear. He cannot see how it all fits together — God, Christ, the cross, resurrection, judge-ment — whatever does it all mean? Another hears and it all fits into place — he understands his need, he sees himself as a sinner, he knows that he is not right before God, he hears of Christ's perfect person and work, he rejoices at Christ's gracious calls to repent and believe in him, and it all makes sense. It is just what he always wanted, just what he desper-ately needs. In John Bunyan's terms, the burden falls off his back. This does not come from a decision based on our unsullied free will. It comes from Christ's breaking through our blindness, ignorance and spiritual deadness in order to give us a true and saving knowledge of himself.

A true and saving knowledge of Christ means that we will recognize that he is **'the true God'** (5:20). The most natural way to understand this startling description is to apply it to **'his Son Jesus Christ'**, not to the Father. It is therefore a clear affirmation of the full deity of Christ. This is something that is taught elsewhere in Scripture (e.g. John 1:1; 20:28; Col. 2:9; Heb. 1:8; Titus 2:13; 2 Peter 1:1), and John says that Christians *know* that it is God's truth. Eternal life is found only in the true God — Jesus Christ who is God's eternal Son.

A warning in conclusion

John's final words are somewhat abrupt: **'Little children, keep yourselves from idols. Amen'** (5:21). In the context of 1 John, the apostle was writing against the Gnostics who denied the incarnation of God's Son. They were not bowing down to wood or stone, but they had a wrong view of God. The Bible teaches that what we covet most in life becomes our god (Col. 3:5). Our god may be fame, fortune, pleasure, a fancy car, or the most impressive house on the street. This shows us that idolatry is not just about kissing statues of the Virgin Mary and the saints. The Gnostics of old were guilty of idolatry. Anybody with a wrong view of God today is guilty of idolatry. Those who worship a god who only loves and never judges are worshipping an idol who exists only in their own imagination. Any view of God which departs from the biblical revelation of him in the God-man Jesus Christ is idolatrous. It is a warning which is as relevant today as it was when it was originally issued in the first century.

John's first epistle was written to give a way of testing true Christianity from false Christianity, and thereby raising the level of assurance in those believers who genuinely belong to the Lord Jesus Christ. The nineteenth-century hymn-writer Daniel Webster Whittle did not know why God's wondrous grace had come to him, nor how faith and peace had come to him, nor how the Spirit brought about a knowledge of Jesus through his Word, nor what was ahead of the Christian in this life, nor when Christ would come again, or Webster himself would die. That did not matter:

But 'I know whom I have believed,
and am persuaded that he is able
to keep that which I've committed
unto him against that day.'

Having worked through 1 John, can you sing that with conviction?

2 John:
An introduction

By the time the apostle John came to write his second and third epistles, he had become so familiar to his readers that he simply called himself 'the elder' (2 John 1; 3 John 1). It is surely significant that Papias of Hierapolis in the early second century referred to the apostles as 'elders'.[1] Writing authoritatively as an apostle — probably the last surviving apostolic eyewitness of Christ — John put together his second epistle, perhaps on a single sheet of papyrus, to encourage Christians to walk in truth and love, and to warn them against false teachers. It was John's desire that grace, mercy and peace would belong to the church (v. 3). To that end, he had to set out both the positive and the negative sides of the Christian faith.

17.
Fellowship in the truth; confronting falsehood

Please read 2 John

The church consists of God's elect

John writes to **'the elect lady and her children'** (v. 1). The lady is probably not a woman (as Alfred Plummer thought)[1] but a church. John writes to 'you' singular in verse 5 and to 'you' plural in verse 6. This is difficult to explain if the lady is a literal woman. In addition, the **'elect sister'** of verse 13 seems to be a sister church, sharing the same faith in the same Lord. Both Testaments personify God's covenant community as a woman (e.g. Hosea 1-3; Eph. 5:25-33; 2 Cor. 11:2; Rev. 19:7-9; 21:2). Hence the children of the lady and her 'elect sister' should be seen as members of the two churches concerned (vv.1,4,13).

Our immediate concern, however, is with the description of the lady as 'elect', or 'chosen' (NIV). This is also how Peter describes the church: 'She who is in Babylon, elect together with you, greets you; and so does Mark my son' (1 Peter 5:13). Paul describes the Colossian Christians as 'the elect of God' (Col. 3:12). How do people become Christians? Do they choose Christ? Yes, they do, but how do they come to choose Christ? Acts 13:48 says that 'As many as had been appointed to eternal life believed.' It is those whom God has appointed, or predestined, to eternal life who come to faith in Jesus Christ.

In referring to 'the elect lady and her children', John is describing the predestined people of God. In the Old Testament, Israel was the chosen nation, not the nation which chose God (Deut. 7:6-8). It is the same with the church in the New Testament. When we hear preachers say, 'God has left the choice to you; salvation is all about choices', they are flying in the face of what God says. As the hymn puts it, the church consists of those who are:

> Elect from every nation,
> Yet one o'er all the earth.

The church is united by truth

John writes to **'the elect lady and her children, whom I love in truth, and not only I, but also all those who have known the truth, because of the truth which abides in us and will be with us for ever'** (vv. 1-2). As we have already seen from 1 John 1:1-4, fellowship must be on the basis of a shared view of the truth. There may be room for some disagreement on secondary issues, such as food laws and holy days (see Rom. 14:1-6), but there can be no disagreement among Christians over issues like the full and sufficient authority of Scripture, the person of the God-man Jesus Christ, the perfection of his atonement, Christ's bodily resurrection and salvation by free grace. Any claim that 'Doctrine divides but experience unites' is contrary to Scripture. John affirms that the right doctrine unites Christians. John does not simply love the elect lady, but loves her (i.e. the church) 'in truth'. Such love is found in all those who know the truth.

As Timothy Dwight puts it:

I love thy kingdom, Lord,
The house of thine abode,
The church our blest Redeemer saved
With his own precious blood.

Those who belong to Christ belong to each other. The Christian feels a deep affinity with all who repent of sin, rest on God's free grace in Christ and seek to love and serve him. Age does not matter, nor social status, nor educational attainments, nor even the period of history to which an individual belongs. The Christian can delight in Augustine's *Confessions,* Bernard of Clairvaux's hymns, Calvin's *Institutes,* Pascal's *Pensées,* or the sermons of Dr Martyn Lloyd-Jones. There is a worldwide and universal fellowship of the true church in the truth.

The church obeys God's commands

Love and obedience are intertwined in the apostle's thought: **'I rejoiced greatly that I have found some of your children walking in truth, as we received commandment from the Father... This is love, that we walk according to his commandments. This is the commandment, that as you have heard from the beginning, you should walk in it'** (vv. 4,6). John has heard that some of the elect lady's children (i.e. some of the church members) were walking in the truth. He may be implying that some of them were unruly, or he may only have known about some of them.

Whatever the case, John experienced great joy that these Christians were walking according to the commandments. We are all very prone to the 'Yes, but ...' mentality. God tells me how to run my family — with love and discipline — and my response is 'Yes, but ...' Being sinners, we can always think of a thousand excuses for not doing what God says. We may meet up with people who profess to be Christians but whose lives are governed by various 'prophecies' which they believe they have received from the Lord. It is the wrong response to say, 'Yes, I know the Bible claims to be perfect and sufficient, but these people are so lively and sincere.' Jesus declares, 'If you love me, keep my commandments' (John 14:15). That should get rid of the 'Yes, but ...' mentality.

The church is characterized by love

The Bible is never afraid of the right kind of emotion. John knows what Christian joy is (v. 4), and he goes on to plead for the sustaining of Christian love (vv. 5-6): **'And now I plead with you, lady, not as though I wrote a new commandment to you, but that which we have had from the beginning: that we love one another. This is love, that we walk according to his commandments. This is the commandment, that as you have heard from the beginning, you should walk in it'** (vv. 5-6). Right from the beginning of their Christian lives, John's readers had known this. In his Gospel, John had recorded Jesus' words: 'A new commandment I give to you, that you love one another; as I have loved you, that you also love one another. By this all will know that you are my disciples, if you have love for one another' (John 13:34-35).

In Scripture, truth and love are married to each other. Love 'does not rejoice in iniquity, but rejoices in the truth' (1 Cor. 13:6). Christians are always to speak the truth in love and so grow up into Christ (Eph. 4:15). When these two concepts are divorced, the result is disastrous. Love without truth is sentimentality; truth without love is oppression. What God demands of us is not a bit of love and a bit of truth, but love and truth in all their fulness. What modern society so often separates, the Bible joins together. 'He who loves another has fulfilled the law. For the commandments, "You shall not commit adultery," "You shall not murder," "You shall not steal," "You shall not bear false witness," "You shall not covet," and if there is any other commandment, are all summed up in this saying, namely, "You shall love your neighbour as yourself." Love does no harm to a neighbour; therefore love is the fulfilment of the law' (Rom. 13:8-10). Love is one of the crucial proofs that we know the God who is love.

God's elect are united in the truth, they obey the truth and they love those who are of the truth. Drawing on his own sad experiences, Francis Schaeffer has told of the turmoil in American Presbyterian circles in the 1930s when there was a justifiable separation from the mainstream Presbyterian Church, but then an unhappy split within the ranks of the separatists over premillennialism and whether alcoholic beverages were allowed. Eventually, two separatist churches were formed — the Orthodox Presbyterian Church and the Bible Presbyterian Church. Schaeffer joined the latter group, but came to regret some of the features of the separatists, especially their attitude to true brethren who did not join them. Schaeffer attributed this attitude to pride — an easy trap to fall into — and claimed that 'What was left was frequently a turning inward, a self-righteousness, a hardness.'[2] The lesson is that the church is not only marked by a commitment to truth, but also by obedience and love. If we are children of the elect lady, these three features will characterize our lives too.

Beware of false teachers

The approach of the dawn of the third millennium has seen discernment fly out of the Christian window. Paul tells us that there is a gift of discerning the spirits (1 Cor. 12:10) and John in his first epistle called upon Christians to test the spirits

(1 John 4:1). But today every latest 'Christian' fad is applauded by a gullible church. Human susceptibility to error is the reason for John's writing: **'For many deceivers have gone out into the world who do not confess Jesus Christ as coming in the flesh. This is a deceiver and an antichrist'** (v. 7). We are not used to such strong words today. John says that there are *many* deceivers. They do not constitute a fringe element on the edges of Christendom. Our Lord himself declared that 'Not everyone who says to me, "Lord, Lord," shall enter the kingdom of heaven, but he who does the will of my Father in heaven. Many will say to me in that day, "Lord, Lord, have we not prophesied in your name, cast out demons in your name, and done many wonders in your name?" And then I will declare to them, "I never knew you; depart from me, you who practise lawlessness!" ' (Matt. 7:21-23).

There will be health-and-wealth preachers who have appeared on television and gained a wide audience, yet they do not belong to Christ. These teachers are false, and they have led many astray. In John's day the problem was Docetism — the teaching that Jesus Christ was not a true man. According to this teaching, Christ is one who came as a spirit upon the man Jesus at the baptism, then left before the crucifixion. John bluntly states that a teacher of this doctrine is an antichrist and a deceiver — not that he sees himself in those terms.

To have the Son is to have the Father: **'Whoever transgresses and does not abide in the doctrine of Christ does not have God. He who abides in the doctrine of Christ has both the Father and the Son'** (v. 9). The one who transgresses is the one who 'runs ahead', as the NIV puts it. He wants to go beyond what is written in Scripture (1 Cor. 4:6-7). Almost invariably, heretics see themselves as progressives, as those who are advanced thinkers, ahead of their time, the ones who are placed on this earth to make the Christian message relevant to the present generation. Like the Athenians of old, they love to hear and tell of nothing else but 'some new thing' (Acts 17:21). Orthodox Christianity — assuming it is under-stood at all — is dismissed as dull and boring and out of touch with the times.

In his own cautious way C. H. Dodd espoused just such a heresy. He wrote of the need to maintain loyalty to what he called 'the fundamental truths of the Gospel', but then added: 'Where that loyalty exists, it is possible (as indeed the example of 1 John shows) to embark upon far-reaching reinterpretations of Christian doctrine, and in doing so to enrich its content without obscuring its central purport. It must, however, be admitted that the writer has incautiously expressed himself in terms which might seem to stigmatize any kind of "advance" as disloyalty to the faith, and so to condemn Christian theol-ogy to lasting sterility. This extreme position has not in fact been taken by any of the great Christian communions, how-ever strongly they have emphasized the necessity of maintain-ing the faith which has once for all been delivered to the saints (Jude 3).'[3] Heretics since C. H. Dodd's day have been even less inclined to pay lip-service to the historic Christian faith.

But in running ahead of the Christ who is revealed in the Bible, these people have actually lost touch with God! John had already stated in his first epistle that 'Whoever denies the Son does not have the Father either; he who acknowledges the Son has the Father also' (1 John 2:23). Christ is the only mediator between God and man (1 Tim. 2:5), the one name under heaven given among men by which we must be saved (Acts 4:12) and the one who has declared the Father (John 1:18). If we have seen Christ, we have seen the Father (John 14:9) for the fulness of the Godhead dwells bodily in him (Col. 2:9). It is a sad fact today that so many who teach university courses on religious studies, or who sit on episcopal thrones, or who head up television ministries which are invariably named after themselves, or who write light little works which are supposed to reveal some hitherto hidden spiritual truth, stand condemned by these words from 2 John.

The Christian needs to be awake in spiritual matters: **'Look to yourselves, that we do not lose those things we worked for, but that we may receive a full reward'** (v. 8). The NKJV's translation is that *'we* may not lose those things *we* worked for, but that *we* may receive a full reward';⁴ the NASB has that *'you* might not lose what *we* have accomplished, but that *you* may receive a full reward'; the NIV has that *'you* do not lose what *you* have worked for, but that *you* may be rewarded fully'. The NIV may be the most convincing translation but, whatever the case, a lack of discernment means a loss of some kind or another. A person who is soft on heresy will suffer spiritually. That is why Christ himself has warned us, 'Take heed that no one deceives you' (Mark 13:5). 'For false christs and false prophets will rise and show signs and wonders to deceive, if possible, even the elect. But take heed; see, I have told you all things beforehand' (Mark 13:22-23). To be gullible is to be unfaithful to Christ. 'Watch out' is a pertinent call in today's Christian world. We need a critical spirit which is informed by God's Word and tempered by the Spirit's gift of love.

Do not fall for the cry that 'God's Spirit speaks to our spirits, not our minds.' We are to love God with all our faculties — heart, soul, *mind* and strength (Mark 12:30). The apostle Paul prayed that the love of the Philippians would 'abound still more and more in knowledge and all discernment' (Phil. 1:9). To be stirred up by nothing but emotion, speculation, entertainment and human manipulation is to betray the gospel. 'Watch out!'

A Christian must have no fellowship with false teachers. **'If anyone comes to you and does not bring this doctrine, do not receive him into your house nor greet him; for he who greets him shares in his evil deeds'** (vv. 10-11). 1995 was proclaimed the Year of Tolerance, and it is widely believed that tolerance is a Christian virtue — indeed, the first, and perhaps the only, Christian virtue. This is not so! The Bible places a concern for truth above the supposed virtues of tolerance. It is true that we are not to forget to entertain strangers, for by so doing some have unwittingly entertained angels (Heb. 13:2; see also Gen. 18; Matt. 25:35; Rom. 12:13; 1 Tim. 3:2; 1 Peter 4:9). Yet hospitality must not become a means for undermining God's truth. A document from the early church, known as the *Didache*, sets out as a rule of thumb that Christians should not accept missioners who stay longer than two days or who ask for money.[5]

Referring to John's words, C. H. Dodd lamented that 'We must doubt whether this policy in the end best serves the cause of truth and love, upon which our author lays such stress.' He declined to accept John's ruling here as a sufficient guide to Christian conduct.[6] William Barclay agreed with Dodd, adding rather patronizingly, 'We may recognize the necessity of this way of action in the situation in which John and his people found themselves without in the least holding that we must treat mistaken thinkers in the same way.'[7] To offer fellowship to heretics, however, is to confirm them in their heresy. That kind of charity does harm — harm which may prove to be everlasting.

John is not necessarily saying — as many evangelicals contend — that we should not receive Jehovah's Witnesses and the like into our homes. We need to remember that churches in the first century did not meet in buildings designed for public worship but in houses (see Rom. 16:5; 1 Cor. 16:19; Col. 4:15; Philem. 2). In its context, John's prohibition is not directed at giving the heretic a cup of tea in one's house but at receiving him into the church. It is against accepting him as a Christian and fellowshipping with him, and so providing him with a springboard for action. In short, Christians are not to pretend that heretics are fellow Christians. To tolerate error is to share in error, as verse 11 makes plain. After giving a depressing list of human depravities in Romans 1, Paul condemns those 'who, knowing the righteous judgement of God, that those who practise such things are deserving of death, not only do the same but also approve of those who practise them' (Rom. 1:32). One of the Gnostics of the second century, Marcion, once asked Polycarp of Smyrna, 'Do you recognize me?' Polycarp replied, 'I recognize you as the first-born of Satan.'⁸ So much for open-ended tolerance! The Christian view is that there is such a thing as truth and such a thing as error. To have fellowship with error is to condone and encourage it. It is not being unloving to avoid Kenneth Copeland and Barbara Thiering; it is being faithful.

John had other things to say to the elect lady, but his papyrus had run out. **'Having many things to write to you, I did not wish to do so with paper and ink; but I hope to come to you and speak face to face, that our joy may be full. The children of your elect sister greet you. Amen'** (vv. 12-13). John wanted to speak with his readers face to face — literally, 'mouth to mouth'. If you have a difficulty with someone, it is usually a good practice to meet with him or her personally. I once refused over the phone to remarry a divorcee who had simply left her first husband and wanted to marry another. In so doing, I took a short cut, and it was a mistake. This woman, whom I had never met, deeply resented the refusal. I may have made things easier had I met her and explained the biblical teaching on marriage and divorce. John realizes that there is nothing like being there. That is why, except in extraordinary circumstances, television church is not really church. All human relationships, including fellowship between Christians, are best conducted person-to-person.

3 John:
An introduction

John's third epistle revolves around four men — John himself, Gaius (the man to whom he was writing), Diotrephes (who was bullying the church) and Demetrius (who had borne a good testimony). John says most about Gaius, but we can only know Gaius from what is revealed here. Alfred Plummer has written that Gaius was perhaps the most common name in the Roman Empire,[1] and I. Howard Marshall compares it to John or James today.[2] There is a man named Gaius at Corinth, referred to in Romans 16:23, and there is a Gaius who is stated to have been caught up with the riot at Ephesus (Acts 19:29). Another Gaius is mentioned in Acts 20:4, but we have no way of knowing if any of them can be identified with the Gaius of 3 John. What we do know is that Gaius was beloved as a Christian to John, whereas Diotrephes was causing him some grief.

18.
Contrasting testimonies

Please read 3 John

The Christian is to be concerned with the whole person

This is a point that should not be underestimated in importance: **'Beloved, I pray that you may prosper in all things and be in health, just as your soul prospers. For I rejoiced greatly when brethren came and testified of the truth that is in you, just as you walk in the truth. I have no greater joy than to hear that my children walk in truth'** (vv. 2-4). The apostle John was concerned for Gaius' well-being, which included his health as well as his spiritual growth. This has nothing to do with the modern-day prosperity gospel, with its emphasis on health and wealth, but simply reflects John's concern for the body and soul of his Christian brother. Like Timothy (1 Tim. 5:23), Gaius may not have enjoyed the best of health. C. S. Lewis' *The Screwtape Letters* reveals just how the devil can work, even in spiritual matters. In one of the letters, Screwtape, the senior devil, gives Wormwood, the junior devil, some advice about how he can render quite innocuous the prayers for his mother uttered by his Christian target (or 'patient' as Wormwood calls him): 'Make sure that they are always very "spiritual", that he is always concerned with the state of her soul and never with her rheumatism.'[1] This is a temptation which is designed to make us spiritual in a Platonic, not a biblical, sense. We must never forget that God made us body and soul, and he redeems his people body and soul.

When the Good Samaritan found the battered Jew by the side of the road, he helped him in a physical way — he cared for him, bound his wounds and had him fed and provided for (Luke 10:25-37). He did not seize the opportunity to explain the gospel to him and then tuck a tract into his shirt-pocket! No, for while we are spiritual beings, we are not *only* spiritual beings. It is the deceivers and antichrists who claim that Jesus Christ did not come in the flesh (2 John 7). Christ's body is real; our bodies are real too.

Having said that, John is nevertheless most concerned for the soul too, as verses 3-4 make clear. John has a true pastoral heart. Nothing should excite a Christian more than to hear that others have embraced Christ by faith and are living for him. The same spirit is found in the apostle Paul, who describes himself as a nursing mother and a father to the Thessalonian church (1 Thess. 2:7,11). Bear with this long quotation, but feel the heartbeat behind the words of Paul from 1 Thessalonians 3:1-10:

> Therefore, when we could no longer endure it, we thought it good to be left in Athens alone, and sent Timothy, our brother and minister of God, and our fellow labourer in the gospel of Christ, to establish you and encourage you concerning your faith, that no one should be shaken by these afflictions; for you yourselves know that we are appointed to this. For, in fact, we told you before when we were with you that we would suffer tribulation, just as it happened, and you know. For this reason, when I could no longer endure it, I sent to know your faith, lest by some means the tempter had tempted you, and our labour might be in vain.

But now that Timothy has come to us from you, and brought us good news of your faith and love, and that you always have good remembrance of us, greatly desiring to see us, as we also to see you — therefore, brethren, in all our affliction and distress we were comforted concerning you by your faith. For now we live, if you stand fast in the Lord. For what thanks can we render to God for you, for all the joy with which we rejoice for your sake before our God, night and day praying exceedingly that we may see your face and perfect what is lacking in your faith?

For Paul, it was life itself to know that new converts to Christ were standing firm in the Lord. What a heart for the gospel! Such love for Christ and for his people! We need the same love that we see exhibited here in Paul and John — a heartfelt concern for the whole person, body and soul.

The Christian is to be hospitable to God's people

Inns in the ancient world had a deserved reputation for being unsavoury, so it was doubly important for Christians to show hospitality to their fellow Christians, especially those involved in active ministry. This charge is made very clear in verses 5-6: **'Beloved, you do faithfully whatever you do for the brethren and for strangers, who have borne witness of your love before the church. If you send them forward on their journey in a manner worthy of God, you will do well.'** What claim did these travelling evangelists have on Gaius? Only that they were of the truth and that they were fellow believers. The world may count this as nothing, but not so the Lord Jesus Christ. When he comes again, he will say to his saved sheep: '"Come, you blessed of my Father, inherit the kingdom prepared for you from the foundation of the world: for I was hungry and you gave me food; I was thirsty and you gave me drink; I was a stranger and you took me in; I was naked and you clothed me; I was sick and you visited me; I was in prison and you came to me." Then the righteous will answer him, saying, "Lord, when did we see you hungry and feed you, or thirsty and give you drink? When did we see you a stranger and take you in, or naked and clothe you? Or when did we see you sick, or in prison, and come to you?" And the King will answer and say to them, "Assuredly, I say to you, inasmuch as you did it to one of the least of these my brethren, you did it to me" ' (Matt. 25:34-40).

The least of Christ's brethren are the least of his people. Show hospitality to them and you show hospitality to Christ himself. Indeed, as we saw in our study of 2 John, Christians are to practise hospitality without grumbling, and in doing so may entertain angels without knowing it! (see Rom. 12:13; 1 Peter 4:9; Heb. 13:2). We find hospitality shown to the apostle Paul throughout his evangelistic career (see Acts 16:15; 17:7; 21:8,16; Rom. 16:23). Gaius had shown the same consideration to travelling preachers. He had put himself out; he had suffered inconvenience to his home; his daily routine was disturbed by visitors; his family was rearranged for the sake of furthering the gospel. All this cost Gaius something. It is not the sort of Christian work that receives much applause — it is not like performing miracles or leading the singing. Yet Scripture does not belittle it: 'If you send them forward on their journey in a manner worthy of God, you will do well' (v. 6).

Reasons for supporting Christian missionaries and evangelists

Like the apostle Paul (1 Cor. 9:1-18), John gives a number of reasons for Christians to support those who labour to proclaim the gospel in other places.

1. Missionaries and evangelists work in Christ's name: **'They went forth for his name's sake'** (v. 7). What they are doing is seeking to make Christ known. A Christian cannot possibly be indifferent to such work. One of the daily pressures on the apostle Paul was his deep concern for all the churches (2 Cor. 11:28). Reader, do you find within your heart a deep concern for the cause of Christ in all parts of the world?

2. Missionaries and evangelists are released from any temptation to solicit support from unbelievers: **'taking nothing from the Gentiles'** (v. 7) An unbeliever may willingly give money to Christian causes — that is his business — but Christians must never solicit money from unbelievers. Stewardship campaigns which try to extract finances from the unregenerate are an affront to God. Nothing should be done to make the church financially dependent on non-Christians. As Jesus declared to the twelve disciples, 'Freely you have received, freely give' (Matt. 10:8). People are to first give themselves to the Lord, and then to his workers by the will of God (2 Cor. 8:5). Christian work must be based on *Christian* giving.

3. We become fellow workers in the cause of the gospel. As John says, **'We therefore ought to receive such, that we may become fellow workers for the truth'** (v. 8). Not everyone who professes to be a Christian evangelist is to be welcomed (2 John 10-11). The prelude to the expulsion of J. Gresham Machen from the Presbyterian Church in the USA in 1935-6 was his refusal to support his church's liberal missionaries.[2] We ought never to give money to support liberal and ecumenical causes. But true missionaries of the cross should be supported heartily by Christians: 'He who receives a prophet in the name of a prophet shall receive a prophet's reward. And he who receives a righteous man in the name of a righteous man shall receive a righteous man's reward' (Matt. 10:41). The pioneering Baptist missionary William Carey went to India in 1793, and spent the rest of his life there, till his death in 1834. Despite the difficulties which he faced, Carey was humble enough to appreciate those at home who supported his work. He called them 'ropeholders', those who held the ropes while he was venturing down what he described as a gold-mine in India. We may or may not be in the front line of battle, but we can share in the Lord's work if we support those who are.

The sin of vanity

What is evil highlights what is good, and vice versa. The contrast between Diotrephes and Demetrius brings together an evil example and a good example, that we might shun the one and imitate the other. Diotrephes' sin appears to be more along the lines of vanity and personal ambition than heresy: **'I wrote to the church, but Diotrephes, who loves to have the preeminence among them, does not receive us. Therefore, if I come, I will call to mind his deeds which he does, prating against us with malicious words. And not content with that, he himself does not receive the brethren, and forbids those who wish to, putting them out of the church'** (vv. 9-10). This is a sin which is neither peculiarly ancient nor modern but perennial. There are people who love to be first, to be regarded as pre-eminent. The church just becomes a stage upon which they may strut and so gain applause and prestige. The Scripture makes it clear that Christ alone is to have the pre-eminence in the church (Col. 1:18).

Diotrephes rejected what John had written (v. 9). This is probably another letter rather than 2 John, unless Diotrephes was prepared to tolerate heresy in order to further his own ends — something which is not unlikely but is not mentioned in 3 John. George G. Findlay has suggested that the name 'Diotrephes' means 'Zeus-reared, nursling of Zeus (the king

of the gods)'. He considers that Diotrephes belonged to the
Greek aristocracy.³ Whatever the case, Diotrephes was certainly acting like a Greek aristocrat. His behaviour and attitude flew in the face of the Christian message of humility and
sacrifice. Harnack even considered that Diotrephes was the
first monarchical bishop of Asia!

It must be said, however, that Diotrephes' sin was not so
much his office as his attitude. Our Lord has told us of the
kind of men who are fit to govern his church: 'You know that
the rulers of the Gentiles lord it over them, and those who are
great exercise authority over them. Yet it shall not be so among
you; but whoever desires to become great among you, let him
be your servant. And whoever desires to be first among you,
let him be your slave — just as the Son of Man did not come
to be served, but to serve, and to give his life a ransom for
many' (Matt. 20:25-28). Peter too, as an apostle, warned his
fellow elders: 'Shepherd the flock of God which is among you,
serving as overseers, not by compulsion but willingly, not for
dishonest gain but eagerly; nor as being lords over those en-
trusted to you, but being examples to the flock' (1 Peter 5:2-3).

In contrast to these biblical injunctions, Diotrephes sought
to exalt himself. Specifically, John mentions four sins.

1. Diotrephes *spread malicious gossip* about John.
He might have said that John was too doctrinal, or too
old, or too austere, or behind the times. Who knows?
Any charge will do if power is one's goal. However he
did it, Diotrephes tried to slant people's thinking against
the apostle.

2. Diotrephes *refused to receive Christian brothers*.
Most of these were probably itinerant evangelists. Gaius
received them (see v. 5) but not Diotrephes.

3. Diotrephes *stopped others from receiving these
Christian brothers*. Holding an official position in the

church, Diotrephes used his authority beyond its limits.
A pastor has every right to tell you what God tells you;
he has no right to impose on his people what God has
not imposed.

4. Diotrephes *wrongfully excommunicated people*
who were in fellowship with John.

In these days where virtually all church discipline has broken down, we need to remember that there is such a thing as a
right use of excommunication. Paul called upon the Corinthian
church to expel a member who was guilty of having sexual
relations with his father's wife, presumably his stepmother
(1 Cor. 5). Excommunication is designed to bring about repentance in the offender (1 Cor. 5:5) and protection from moral
pollution for the church (1 Cor. 5:6-7). Those who maintained
that the resurrection is already past — and that there is no
resurrection of the body to come — were also dealt with by
Paul. He handed them over to Satan that they might learn not
to blaspheme (1 Tim. 1:20; 2 Tim. 2:16-18). At the end of the
apostolic period, Christ was to proclaim through John that the
church at Thyatira needed to expel the false prophetess Jez-
ebel who was leading some of the congregation into idolatry
and immorality (Rev. 2:20).

But with Diotrephes, it was not a case of the godly exercise of biblical discipline but a power play. The Bible does not
simply advocate discipline in home and church; it advocates
loving and holy discipline. In one of his letters, Augustine of
Hippo declared, 'One thing I say deliberately as an unques-
tionable truth, that if any believer has been wrongfully excommunicated, the sentence will do harm rather to him who pro-
nounces it than to him who suffers this wrong. For it is by the
Holy Spirit dwelling in holy persons that anyone is loosed or
bound, and he inflicts unmerited punishment upon no one; for
by him the love which works not evil is shed abroad in our

hearts.'⁴ Diotrephes' sin was not heresy, fiddling the books, or adultery; it was uncontrolled vanity. How common this is! We want people to take notice of us, to think that we are somebody — and as a result we lose Jesus' perspective on true greatness.

The blessing of a good example

John is happy to commend the example of Demetrius: **'Beloved, do not imitate what is evil, but what is good. He who does good is of God, but he who does evil has not seen God. Demetrius has a good testimony from all, and from the truth itself. And we also bear witness, and you know that our testimony is true'** (vv. 11-12). We are all natural imitators; we tend to become like the people we are with. That is why we need the warning of the apostle Paul: 'Do not be deceived: "Evil company corrupts good habits" ' (1 Cor. 15:33). If we mix with people who are foul-mouthed louts, we will become like them. The question is not 'Will we imitate?' but 'Whom will we imitate?' John tells us not to imitate those who are puffed up with their own importance, who are pushy and self-assertive like Diotrephes, but to imitate a man like Demetrius who is good (see too 1 Cor. 11:1; 2 Thess. 3:7; Heb. 6:12; 13:7).

Demetrius expressed in the flesh something of the goodness of God — he is not a perfect example, of course, but he is a good example. John says that all people can see this (v. 12). Despite Howard Marshall's view,⁵ it seems that John means more than that all Christians can see this. By God's common grace, even unbelievers can recognize it too. This is a biblical notion. Regarding the qualifications for an elder/overseer, Paul says, 'Moreover he must have a good testimony among those who are outside, lest he fall into reproach and the snare of the

devil' (1 Tim. 3:7). The non-Christian has not lost all capacity
to judge what is good and true.

John also declares that Demetrius has a good testimony
'from the truth itself' (v. 12). F. F. Bruce considers that this is
actually 'the Truth himself', the Lord Jesus Christ;[6] Alfred
Plummer considers that it is a reference to the Holy Spirit;[7]
but John Stott considers that John is saying that the genuine-
ness of Demetrius is self-evident.[8] It may simply mean that as
Demetrius commends the faith (as a body of truth), so the
faith commends him. John adds his commendation of
Demetrius, adding that his apostolic testimony to this good
man is to be believed because it is true.

It would be wonderful to think that this Demetrius was the
Demetrius of Acts 19. This Demetrius was a silversmith in
Ephesus who made silver shrines of the goddess Artemis. When
his business came under threat through the preaching of the
apostle Paul, he led a riot against the new faith (Acts 19:24-
29). Unfortunately, we have no way of knowing if the identifi-
cation of the two men of the same name can be made. What
we do know is that the Demetrius of 3 John bore a good testimony; he is one to imitate.

A personal touch

John bids farewell to Gaius: **'I had many things to write,
but I do not wish to write to you with pen and ink; but I
hope to see you shortly, and we shall speak face to face.
Peace to you. Our friends greet you. Greet the friends by
name'** (vv. 13-14). We ought not to underestimate the personal touch. The apostle Paul, for example, had not yet visited
the church at Rome but he still takes time at the end of his
most extensive and systematic epistle to send his greetings to
a number of Christians at Rome, many of whom he names

with deep affection (Rom. 16:1-16). In my own life, I have often regretted that I have met people and have been so quick to forget their names! We need to reflect more of the mind of Christ even in this area. It is not as minor as it might first appear. Christ spoke of himself as the Shepherd of the sheep: 'To him the doorkeeper opens, and the sheep hear his voice; and he calls his own sheep by name and leads them out' (John 10:3). It is good to finish this study on a note of personal affection and Christian peace.

Notes

1 John: An introduction

1. D. Jackman, *The Message of John's Letters,* IVP, 1988, p.18. See also Judith Lieu, *The Theology of the Johannine Epistles,* Cambridge University Press, 1991, p.22; Simon Kistemaker, *James and I-III John,* Baker Book House, 1986, p.218.

2. A. E. Brooke, *A Critical and Exegetical Commentary on the Johannine Epistles,* T. & T. Clark, 1912, reprinted 1980, p.xxxii.

3. D. Martyn Lloyd-Jones, *The Love of God: Studies in 1 John,* vol. 4, Crossway, 1994, p.79.

4. Ignatius of Antioch, *The Epistle to the Smyrnaeans,* 5, in M. Staniforth (trans.), *Early Christian Writings,* Penguin, 1972, p.120.

5. D. Martyn Lloyd-Jones, *Fellowship with God: Studies in 1 John,* vol. 1, Crossway, 1993, p.59.

6. A. A. Hodge, *Evangelical Theology,* Banner of Truth Trust, reprinted 1990, pp.310-11.

7. R. Kent Hughes, *Are Evangelicals Born Again?* Crossway, 1995.

8. Cited in I. Howard Marshall, *The Epistles of John,* Wm B. Eerdmans Pub. Co., 1978, p.xi.

Chapter 1 — The incarnate Word

1. Some commentators think that John is only referring here to the beginning of the community's existence (as in 2:7; 3:11). John is sometimes deliberately ambiguous, but his references are so concrete that he must also be alluding to the person of Christ, not just to the reception of the gospel by the church to which he is writing.

2. P. Cameron, *Fundamentalism and Freedom,* Doubleday, 1995, p.119.

3. See D. Edwards with John Stott, *Essentials,* Hodder and Stoughton, 1990. Stott makes some telling points and is commendably courteous in all his dealings with the liberal Edwards, but the tone is too concessive. We are left with the impression that the debate is taking place within the Christian household, whereas Edwards is in fact denying basic Christian truths. At one point in the debate Stott even declares that those who deny the bodily resurrection of Jesus do not necessarily forfeit the right to be called Christians (p.228) — an obvious departure from Paul's vigorous assertion in 1 Corinthians 15:12-19.

4. A Christian is forbidden to marry a non-Christian (e.g. 1 Cor. 7:39), but must continue, if possible, in a marriage which has already been contracted with an unbeliever (1 Peter 3:1-6; 1 Cor. 7:12-16).

5. Cited in H. E. Hopkins, *Charles Simeon of Cambridge,* Hodder and Stoughton, 1977, p.203.

Chapter 2 — God is light
1. Cited in Hughes, *Are Evangelicals Born Again?* pp.21-2.
2. B. F. Westcott, *The Epistles of John,* MacMillan and Co., 1886, p.36.

Chapter 3 — Dealing with sin
1. J. R. W. Stott, *The Epistles of John,* IVP, 1976, p.79.
2. See F. LaGard Smith, *Out on a Broken Limb,* Harvest House Publishers, 1986, p.179.
3. A. Toplady, *Complete Works,* reprinted by Sprinkle, 1987, pp.448-50.
4. D. Bonhoeffer, *Life Together,* trans. by J. W. Doberstein, SCM, 1972, p.89.
5. N. B. Stonehouse, *J. Gresham Machen: A Biographical Memoir,* Banner of Truth Trust, 1987, p.508.
6. See J. Murray, *Redemption Accomplished and Applied,* Wm B. Eerdmans Pub. Co., 1975, pp.72-5.

Chapter 4 —Two tests
1. J. Calvin, *Commentaries on the Catholic Epistles,* trans. by John Owen, Baker Book House, reprinted 1979, p.175.
2. Ernest C. Reisinger, *Lord and Christ,* Presbyterian and Reformed, 1994, p.40.
3. *The Weekend Australian,* 14-15 January 1995.
4. G. G. Findlay, *Fellowship in the Life Eternal: An Exposition of the Epistles of St John,* James and Klock, reprinted 1977, pp.143-4.
5. H. C. G. Moule, *Charles Simeon,* IVP, reprinted 1965, p.44.
6. K. Grayston, *The Johannine Epistles,* NCB, 1984, pp.12-14.
7. The NIV has 'live' in him, but the word is stronger, and means 'abide' or 'remain'.
8. R. Candlish, *A Commentary on 1 John,* Banner of Truth Trust, 1993 (originally published 1870), pp.99-100.
9. F. Schaeffer, *The Church at the End of the Twentieth Century,* IVP (USA), 1970, appendix II; also published separately.
10. Candlish, *Commentary on 1 John,* p.119.

Chapter 5 — The Christian and the world
1. Two different words for 'little children' are used in verses 12-14 but they are virtually synonymous.
2. David Jackman considers that, although the masculine gender is used, it applies to women and girls too (Jackman, *The Message of John's Letters,* p.55).
3. The NIV has 'lives', which is a little weak.
4. Augustine, *The City of God,* trans. by Henry Bettenson, Penguin, reprinted 1972, XV,7.
5 Cited in A. Vidler, *The Church in an Age of Revolution,* Penguin, 1971, p.278.

Chapter 6 — Beware of antichrists!
1. Cited in D. G. Hart, 'The Princeton Mind in the Modern World and the Common Sense of J. Gresham Machen' in *Westminster Theological Journal*, vol. XLVI, no. 1, Spring 1984, p.3.

Chapter 7 — Living in God's family
1. J. Montgomery Boice, *The Epistles of John*, Zondervan, Michigan, 1979, p.96. Candlish is surely wrong in saying that John was writing about seeing the Father (Candlish, *Commentary on 1 John*, pp.238-9).
2. Candlish, *Commentary on 1 John*, p.280.
3. These words are added in many significant manuscripts and are probably authentic.
4. Cited in J. Adams, *The Biblical View of Self-Esteem, Self-Love, Self-Image*, Harvest House Publishers, 1986, p.91.
5. D. Martyn Lloyd-Jones, *Children of God: Studies in 1 John*, vol. 3, Crossway, 1993, p.22.

Chapter 8 — The child of God and sin
1. *The Shorter Catechism*, Question 14.
2. R. E. Brown, *The Epistles of John*, Doubleday and Co, 1984, p.413.
3. J. Wesley, *Works*, Baker Book House, reprinted 1986, vol. XI, p.367.
4. *Ibid.*, p.446.
5. C. Finney, *Systematic Theology*, Bethany House, reprinted 1994, p.382.
6. *Ibid.*, p.300.
7. *The Shorter Catechism*, Answer to Question 82.
8. Cited in D. W. Frank, *Less Than Conquerors*, Wm B. Eerdmans Pub. Co., 1986, p.242. B. B. Warfield's *Perfectionism* does a demolition job on this kind of teaching.
9. A. Plummer, *The Epistles of St John*, Baker Book House, reprinted 1980, p.77.
10. A. Bonar (ed.), *Memoir and Remains of Robert Murray M'Cheyne*, Banner of Truth Trust, reprinted 1973, p.343.

Chapter 9 — Love one another
1. Cited in T. H. L. Parker, *John Calvin*, Lion, 1977, p.54.
2. A. Moody Stuart, *The Life of John Duncan*, Banner of Truth Trust, reprinted 1991, p.171.

Chapter 10 — Dealing with doubt
1. Candlish, *Commentary on 1 John*, p.346.
2. *Westminster Confession of Faith*, 18.2.
3. Cited by J. R. Beeke in *The Banner of Sovereign Grace Truth*, vol. 3, no. 1, January 1995, p.7.
4. *Ibid.*, p.8.
5. Candlish, *Commentary on 1 John*, p.318.
6. Sinclair Ferguson, *John Owen on the Christian Life*, Banner of Truth Trust, 1987, p.115.
7. Candlish, *A Commentary on 1 John*, p.318.
8. Lloyd-Jones, *Children of God*, p.127.

9. Cited in Ian Ker, *John Henry Newman: A Biography,* Clarendon Press, 1988, p.690.

10. Stuart, *Life of John Duncan,* p.166.

11. Cited in Ferguson, *John Owen on the Christian Life,* p.111.

12. Ferguson, *John Owen on the Christian Life,* p.2.

Chapter 11 — Testing the spirits

1. Wayne Grudem has suggested that the New Testament apostles are the successors to the Old Testament prophets. Prophecy in the New Testament, as opposed to that in the Old Testament, is regarded as more general and less authoritative. He writes, 'Each prophecy might have both true and false elements in it, and those would be sifted and evaluated for what they were' (see W. Grudem, *The Gift of Prophecy in the New Testament and Today,* Kingsway Publications, 1988, p.78). He is then forced to argue that the book of Revelation is an example of uniquely authoritative 'apostolic prophecy' (p.160). This is because Revelation identifies itself as prophecy (Rev. 1:3) and severely warns against adding to the words of the prophecy of the book or taking away from it (Rev. 22:18-19). Grudem ends up with 'prophecy' which would be impossible to evaluate and which detracts, even if only in a somewhat vague way, from the sufficiency of Scripture.

2. J. Adams, *A Call to Discernment,* Harvest House Publishers, 1987, p.15.

3. Cited in J. N. Oswalt, *The Book of Isaiah, Chapters 1-39,* Wm B. Eerdmans Pub. Co., 1986, p.203.

4. This is inadequate. Jesus came to show God's love for sinners; that is true, but the main purpose of his death was to pay the penalty for sin so that God's justice could be satisfied and sinners could obtain mercy from God (see Rom. 3:25-26). The quotation comes from W. Barclay, *Testament of Faith,* Mowbrays, p.52.

5. This scouts around the central issue — that Jesus rose bodily from the dead. The quotation comes from Barclay, *Testament of Faith,* p.108.

6. That sounds very spiritual, but Barclay meant that ultimately everybody would be saved — contrary to the clear teaching of Jesus in, for example, Matthew 25:31-46; Luke 16:19-31 and John 5:28-29. The quotation comes from Barclay, *Testament of Faith,* p.61 (see also p.58).

7. See Irenaeus, *Against Heresies,* I,1,3; I,3,2 and I,3,6. Christ, of course, only remained forty days with his disciples after his resurrection. The Greek word for 'Jesus' begins with an iota (which has the numerical value of 10) and an eta (which has the numerical value of 8).

8. *Letters of John Calvin,* selected from the Bonnet edition, Banner of Truth Trust, 1980, p.144.

9. For example, Galatians 5:2-4 shows that we cannot add to the message of salvation through the free grace of Christ, and 1 Corinthians 6:9-10 shows that the habitual practice of certain sins excludes one from membership in the kingdom of God.

Chapter 12 — Love is of God

1. Augustine, *Ten Homilies on the First Epistle of John,* in *The Nicene and Post-Nicene Fathers,* ed. by P. Schaff, reprinted by Wm B. Eerdmans Pub. Co., 1974, 'The Prologue'.

2. *Ibid.*, VII, 8. Augustine certainly did not mean what the advocates of situation ethics mean — that love abolishes the law of God.
3. 'Him' is missing from a number of important manuscripts. The meaning of the passage as a whole is not drastically altered if 'him' is included or excluded.
4. Candlish, *Commentary on 1 John,* p.380.
5. The NIV is not inaccurate but is a little too vague.
6. Verse 20 concludes with a question in the NKJV, but a statement in most other modern versions. The meaning is the same.
7. B. H. Edwards, *Through Many Dangers,* Evangelical Press, 1994, p.161.
8. For example, 1 John 2:2 has been used to teach universal salvation; Leo Tolstoy used 1 John and the Sermon on the Mount to teach that salvation is by love, not by faith in the atoning work of God's divine Son; from 1 John 2:20,27 some have deduced that there is no need for teachers in the church; and perfectionism has been found in 1 John 3:6,9. Half-truths are the breeding ground for outright heresies.
9. Calvin, *Commentaries on the Catholic Epistles,* pp.248, 245. Calvin, however, regards verses 17-18 as referring to the love of God which we perceive through faith, not our love for God. It is difficult to understand how such love could be perfected.
10. *Ibid.,* p.245.
11. Candlish, *Commentary on 1 John,* p.409.

Chapter 13 — Summarizing the three tests
1. J. Beeke, 'Understanding Assurance: 1' in *Banner of Truth,* Issue 392, May 1996, p.21. The spelling has been modernized. Dr Beeke's second article on assurance is found in Issue 394, July 1996. They are most helpful and highly commended.
2. Cited in J. C. Ryle, *Light From Old Times,* Evangelical Press, 1980, pp.95-6.

Chapter 14 — Belief and unbelief
1. R. L. Dabney, *Discussions: Evangelical and Theological,* Banner of Truth Trust, 1891, reprinted 1982, pp.377-90. Only in the fifth century did some of the Latin Fathers in North Africa and Italy begin to cite the passage (see B. Metzger, *A Textual Commentary on the Greek New Testament,* UBS, 1971, pp.716-18). It is highly significant — indeed, conclusive — that the church in the fourth and fifth centuries formulated her creeds, which set out the doctrines of the Trinity and the deity of Christ, without reference to this passage about the three heavenly witnesses.
2. Rudolf Bultmann maintains that the 'water' and 'blood' of verse 6 are different from the 'water' and 'blood' in verse 8. He says of the latter verse, 'What they now mean can scarcely be in doubt: they are now the sacraments of baptism and the Lord's Supper, which bear testimony for Jesus Christ as God's Son, since they mediate the salvation of the community imparted through him' (R. Bultmann, *The Johannine Epistles,* trans. by R. Philip O'Hara with L. C. McGaughy and R. W. Funk, Fortress Press, 1986, pp.80-81). This is precisely the wrong kind of 'Christian' assurance.
3. R. Candlish, *Commentary on 1 John,* pp.460, 469, 471. Raymond Brown maintains that John was referring to the death of Jesus, although he says that this

is 'not without some obscurity; but it solves more problems than any other theory' (see Brown, *The Epistles of John,* pp.577-8).

4. Boice, *The Epistles of John,* p.164.

5. Stott, *The Epistles of John,* p.178; F. F. Bruce, *The Epistles of John,* Pickering and Inglis, London, 1978, pp.118-19; Marshall, *The Epistles of John,* pp.231-2.

6. Cerinthus believed that the Christ descended on the man Jesus at the baptism and left him just before the crucifixion.

7. Cited in D. Martyn Lloyd-Jones, *Joy Unspeakable,* Kingsway, 1984, p.160.

8. Stott, *The Epistles of John,* p.182.

9. B. Russell, *Why I Am Not a Christian,* George Allen & Unwin, 1975. It is revealing that the philosopher Russell failed completely to tackle the issue of Christ's resurrection from the dead. His dismissal of Christian sexual ethics is obviously related to his own need to rationalize his own misbehaviour.

Chapter 15 — Assurance in the Christian life

1. The last part of the verse probably did not form part of the original epistle that John wrote.

2. H. J. Schroeder (trans.), *Canons and Decrees of the Council of Trent,* Tan Books and Publishers, 1978, p.38.

3. *Ibid.,* p.44.

4. Cited in C. Samuel Storms, *Healing and Holiness,* Presbyterian and Reformed, 1990, p.28.

5. *Ibid.,* p.29. There are a number of verses which demolish the whole 'name it and claim it' approach to prayer (see Dan. 3:16-18; Matt. 26:39-42; Mark 1:40; Acts 12:5-17; James 4:13-15).

6. C. H. Dodd, *The Johannine Epistles,* Hodder and Stoughton, 1946, pp.136-7.

7. E. Bethge, *Dietrich Bonhoeffer,* Collins, 1977, p.389. Bonhoeffer actually meant the Moral Rearmament Oxford Group, not the Anglo-Catholic Oxford Movement of the nineteenth century.

Chapter 16 —Knowing where we stand

1. Martin Luther, *On the Bondage of the Will,* trans. by J. I. Packer and O. R. Johnston, J. Clarke & Co, 1973, p.67.

2. Jackman, *The Message of John's Letters,* p.167.

3. We can be thankful that recent Keswick Conventions have tended to depart quite radically from the teaching on sanctification proclaimed back in 1875 when the conventions first began.

2 John — An introduction

1. Eusebius, *The History of the Church,* III, 39, trans. by G. A. Williamson, Penguin, 1984, p.150.

Chapter 17 — Fellowship in the truth, confronting falsehood

1. Plummer, *The Epistles of St John,* p.132.

2. F. Schaeffer, *The Great Evangelical Disaster,* Crossway, 1984, p.75.

3. Dodd, *The Johannine Epistles,* p.150.

4. This idea is found in Galatians 4:11 and Philippians 2:16.

5. *Didache,* 11, in Staniforth (trans.), *Early Christian Writings,* p.233.

6. Dodd, *The Johannine Epistles,* pp.151-2.

7. W. Barclay, *The Letters of John and Jude,* Saint Andrew Press, 1965, p.169.

8. Irenaeus, *Against Heresies,* III, 3 in *The Ante-Nicene Fathers,* vol. 1, reprinted by Wm B. Eerdmans Pub. Co., 1981. The quotation has been slightly modernized. Marcion was not a classic Gnostic in that he did not indulge in Gnostic speculations, but he was a dualist who rejected the Bible's teaching on God as Creator who is also the God and Father of our Lord Jesus Christ.

3 John — An introduction

1. Plummer, *The Epistles of St John,* p.144.

2. Marshall, *The Epistles of John,* p.81.

Chapter 18 — Contrasting testimonies

1. C. S. Lewis, *The Screwtape Letters,* Collins, 1942, Letter III, p.21.

2. Stonehouse, *J. Gresham Machen,* pp.469-92.

3. G. G. Findlay, *Fellowship in the Life Eternal: An Exposition of the Epistles of St. John,* James and Klock, 1909, reprinted 1977, p.41.

4. Augustine, *Nicene and Post-Nicene Fathers,* vol. 1, reprinted by T & T Clark/ Wm B. Eerdmans Pub. Co., Letter CCL, p.590.

5. Marshall, *The Epistles of John,* p.93.

6. Bruce, *The Epistles of John,* p.155.

7. Plummer, *The Epistles of St John,* p.151.

8. Stott, *The Epistles of John,* p.229.